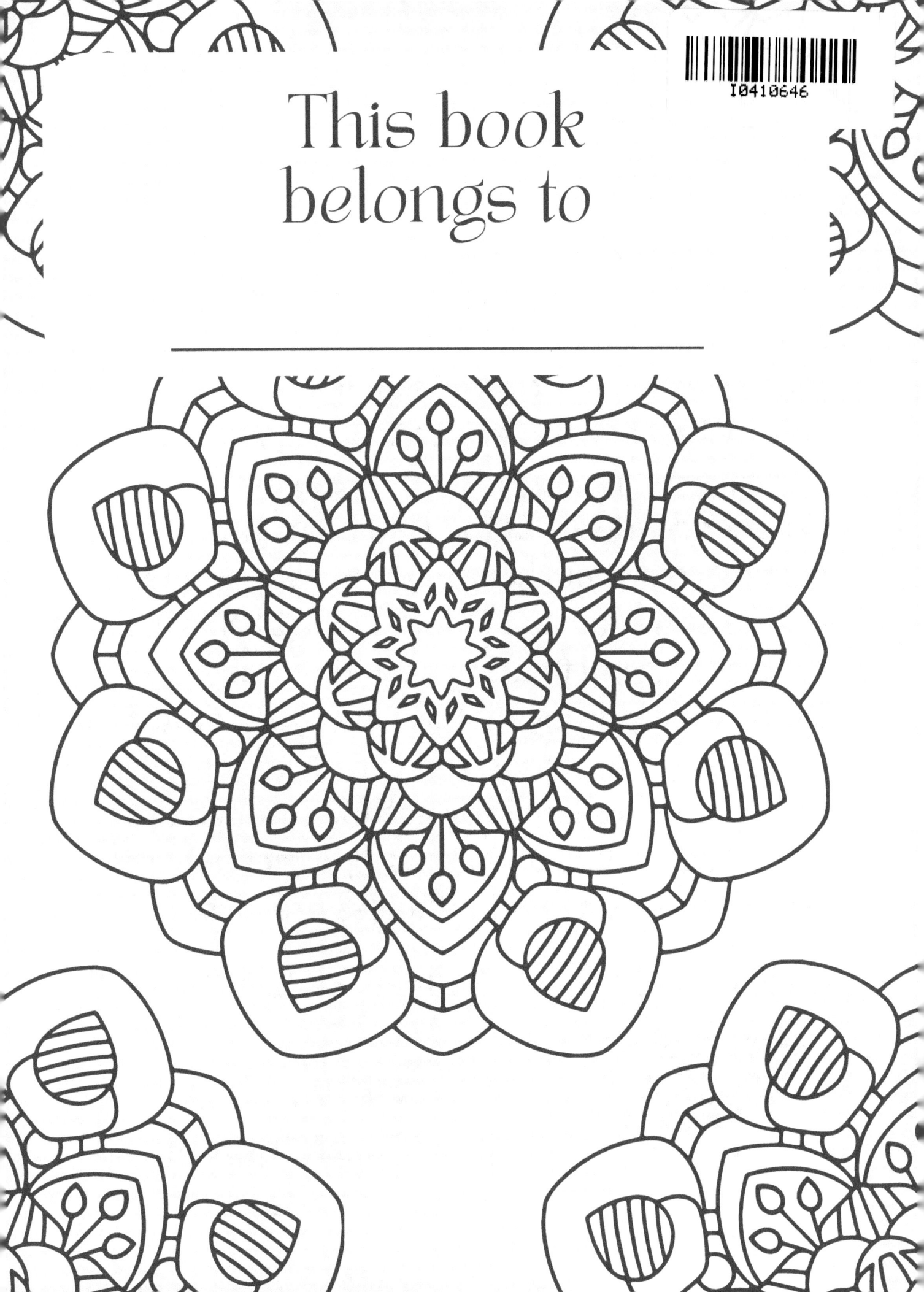

This book
belongs to

_____

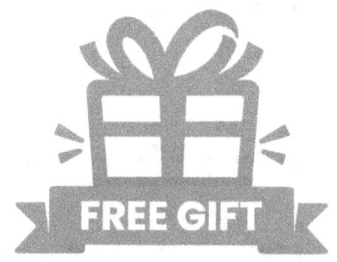

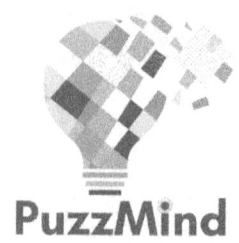

PuzzMind

Step into a world where labyrinthine challenges become the key to unlocking mindfulness and stress relief. Our exclusive offer of 51 maze puzzles with solutions, available for download, is your ticket to a calmer mind. Engage in the intricate paths and twists of these puzzles to experience the art of focused concentration, guiding your thoughts away from stress and into a state of tranquility. Embrace the thrill of solving each puzzle and find solace in the process – a captivating journey that will lead you towards a more serene and centered you. Scan the QR code and embark on a mindful escape through the winding corridors of our maze puzzles, where stress retreats and mindfulness prevails.

https://puzzmind.com/xtras/U2FsdGVkX1.pdf

Write to
info@PuzzMind.com
for more freebies

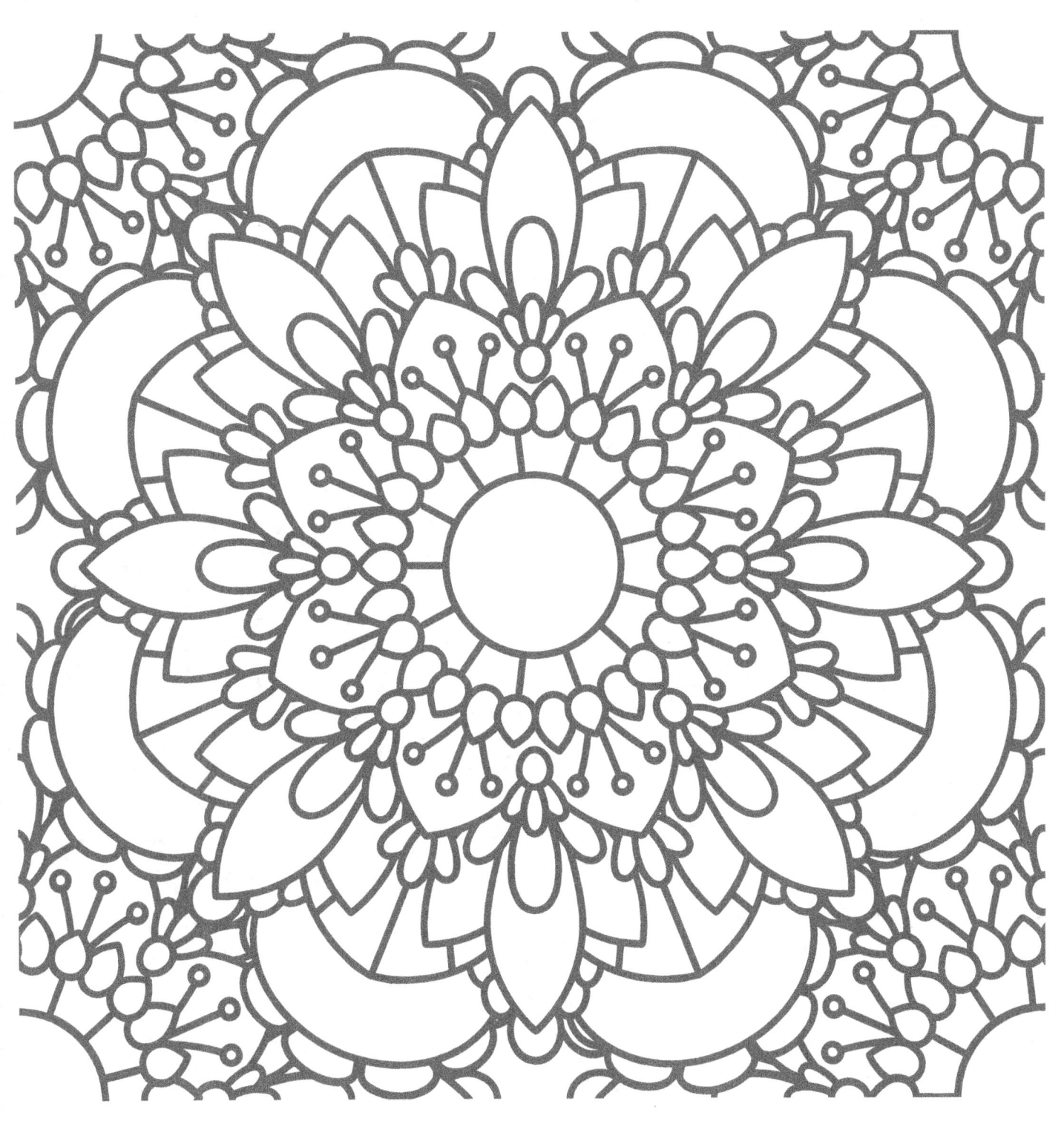

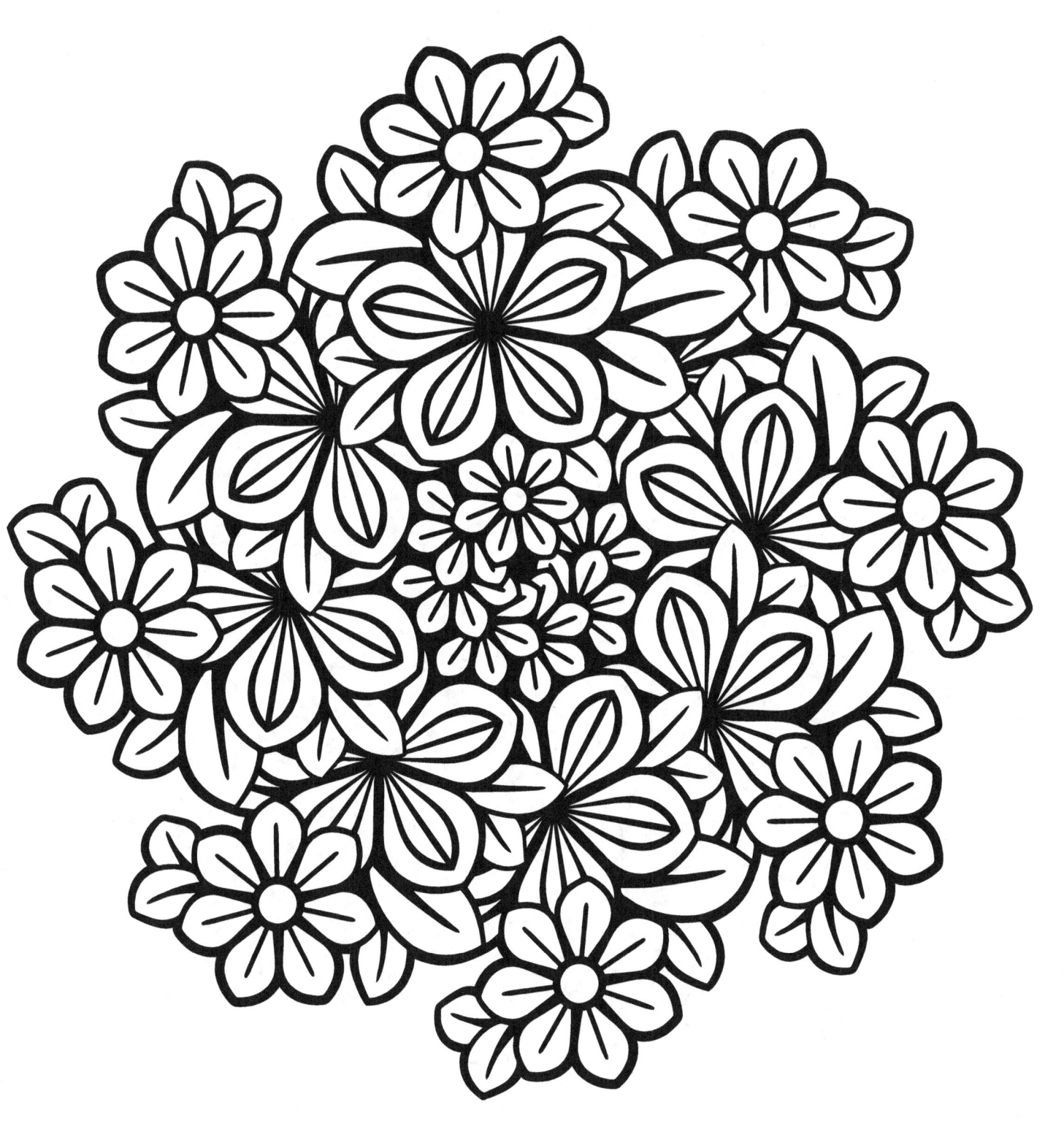

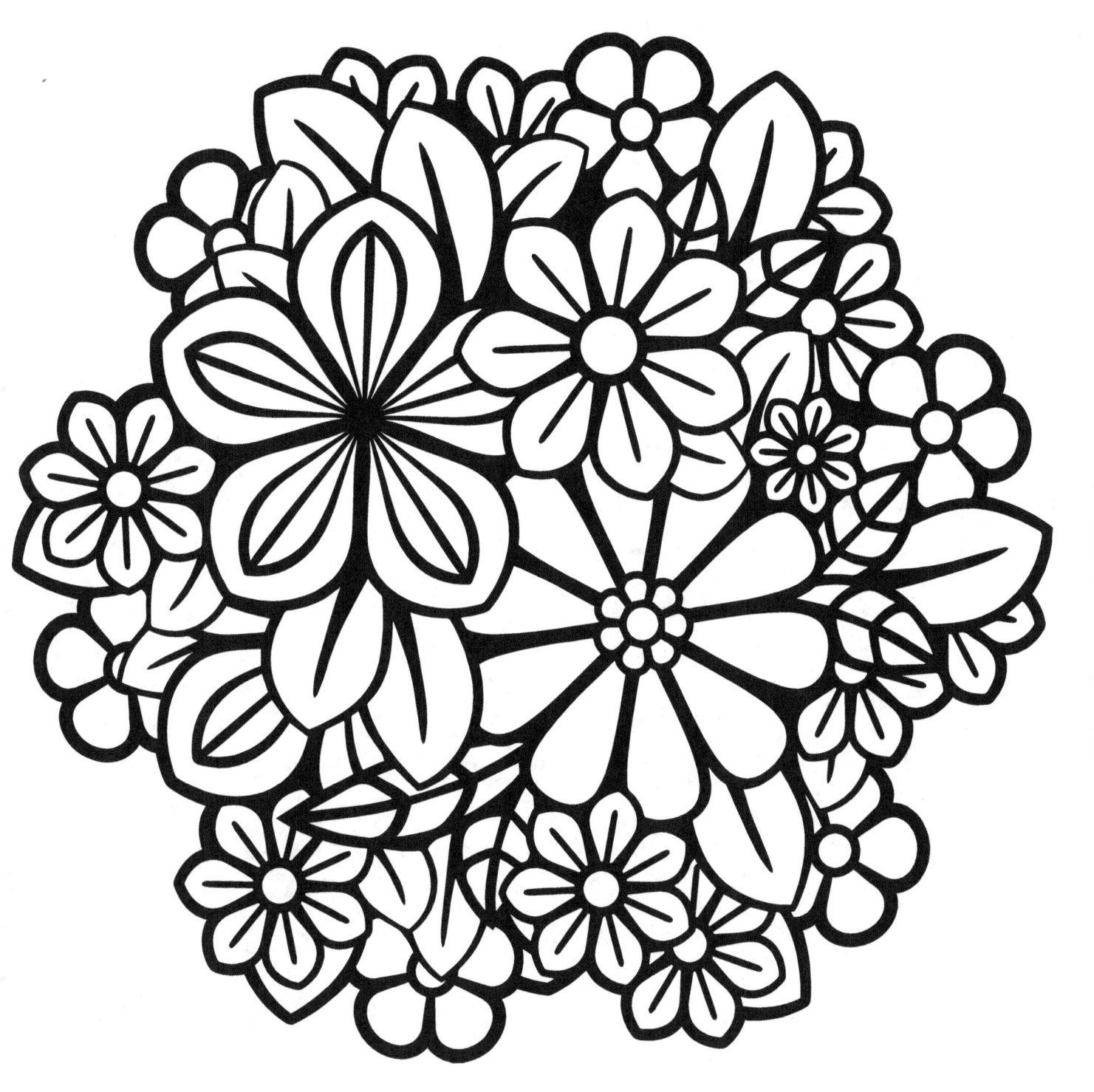

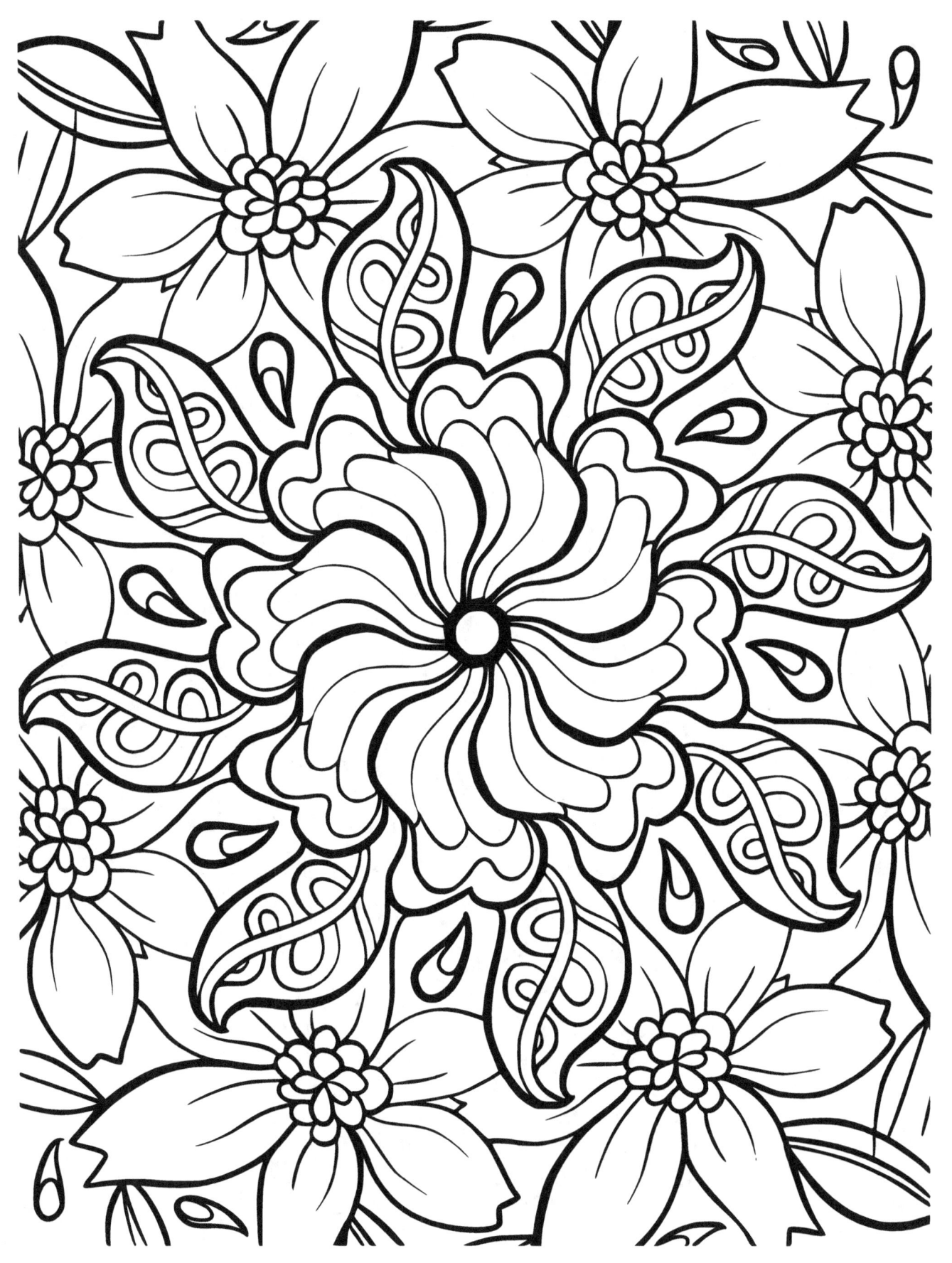

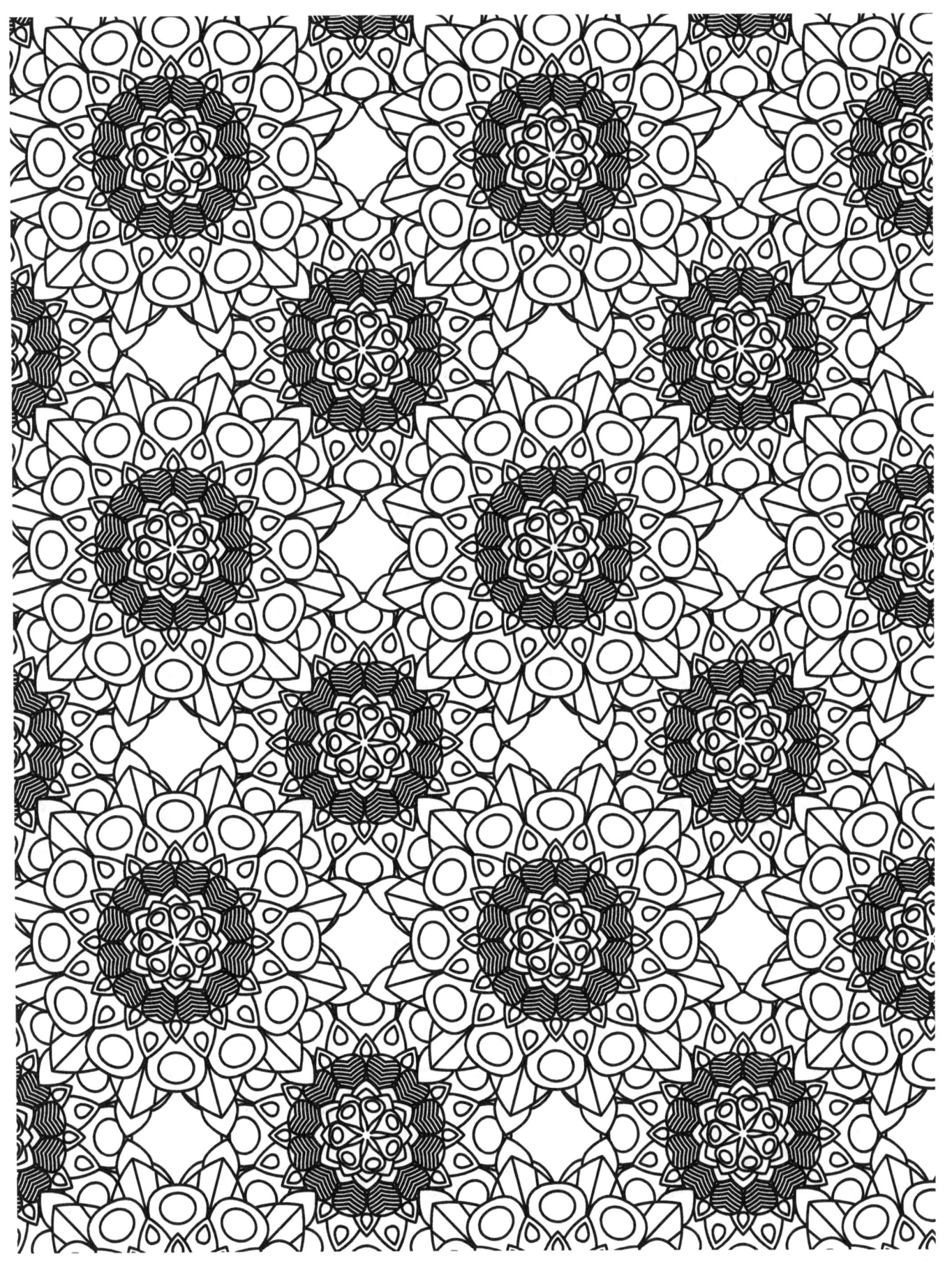

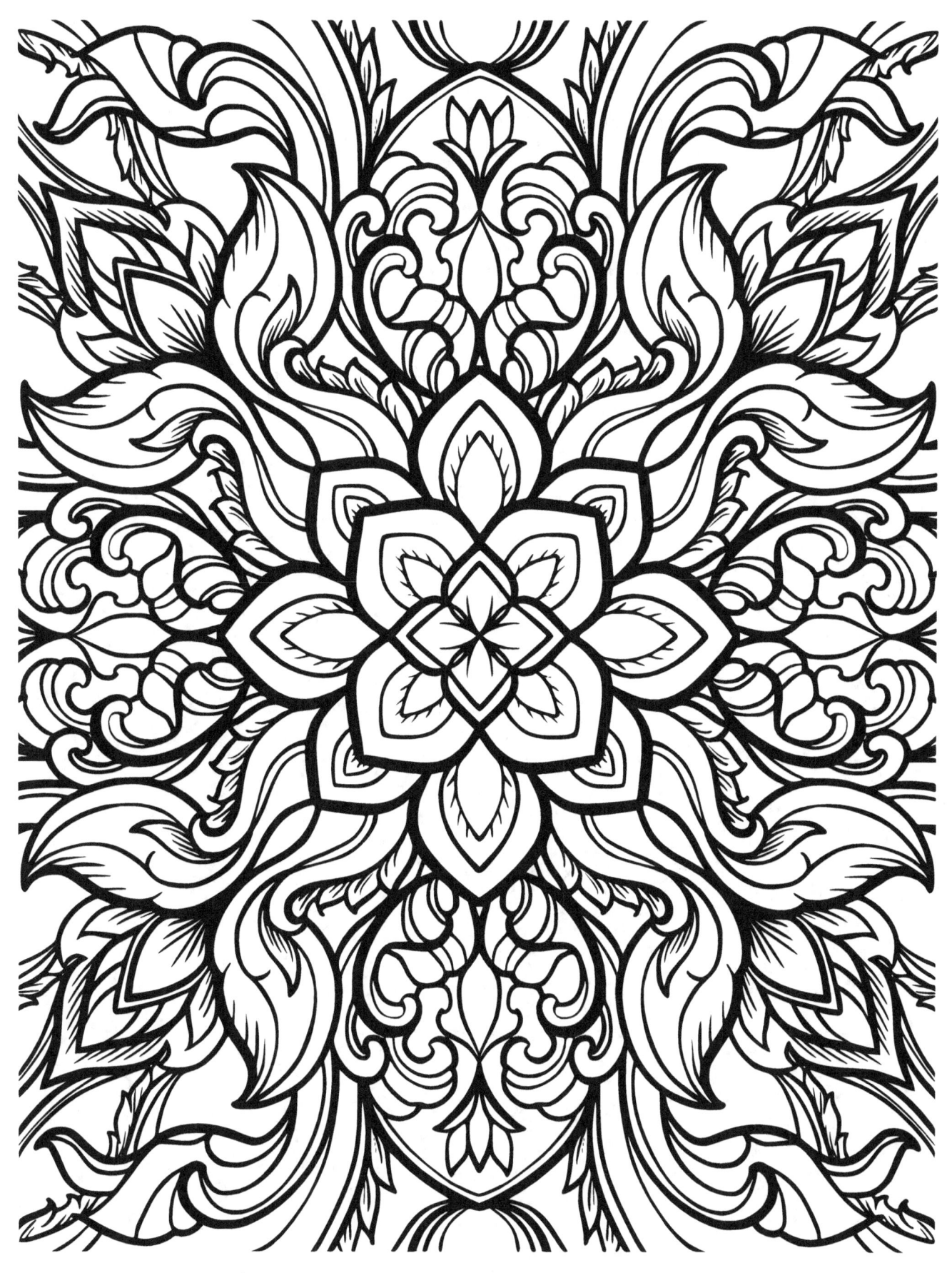

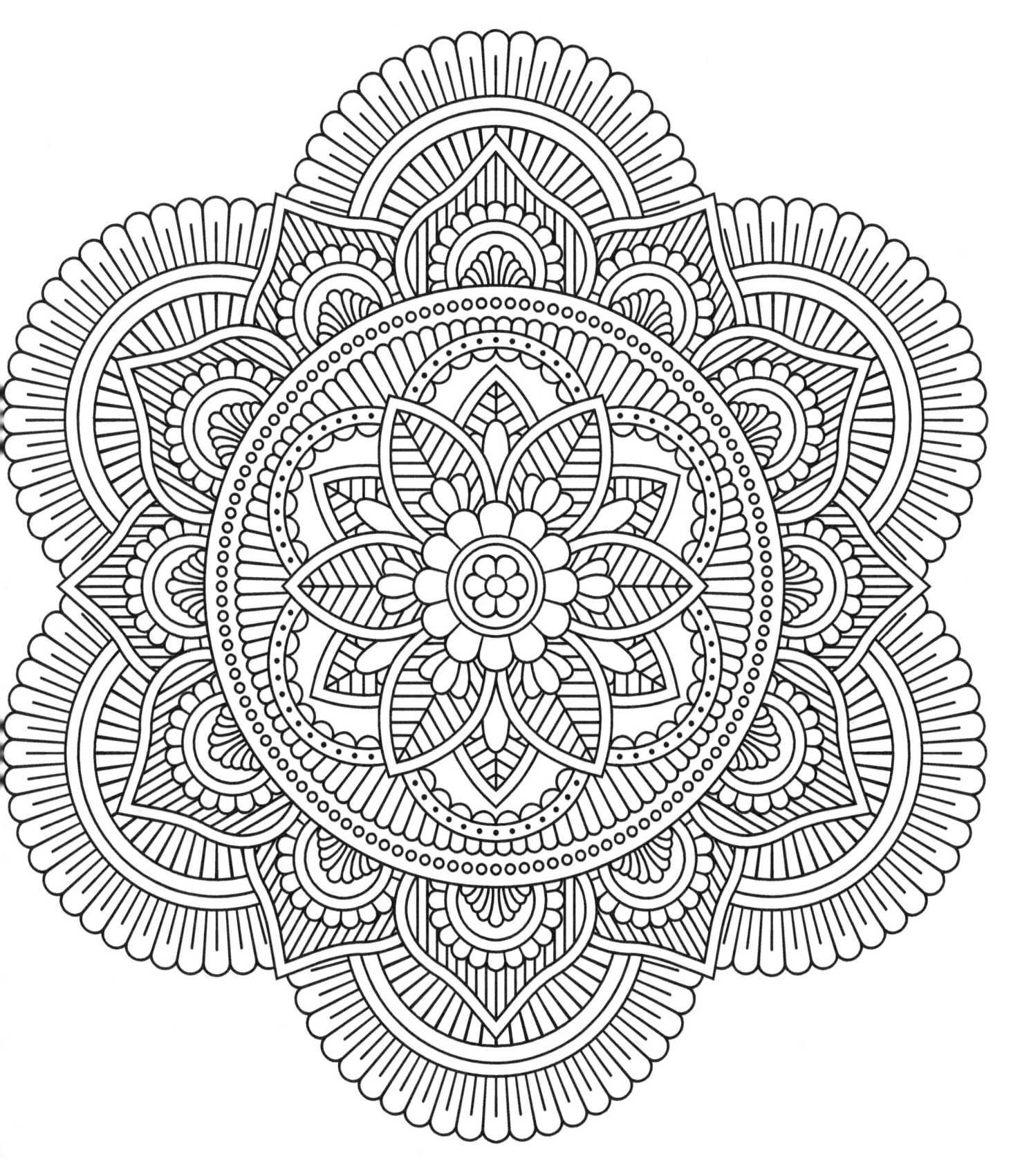

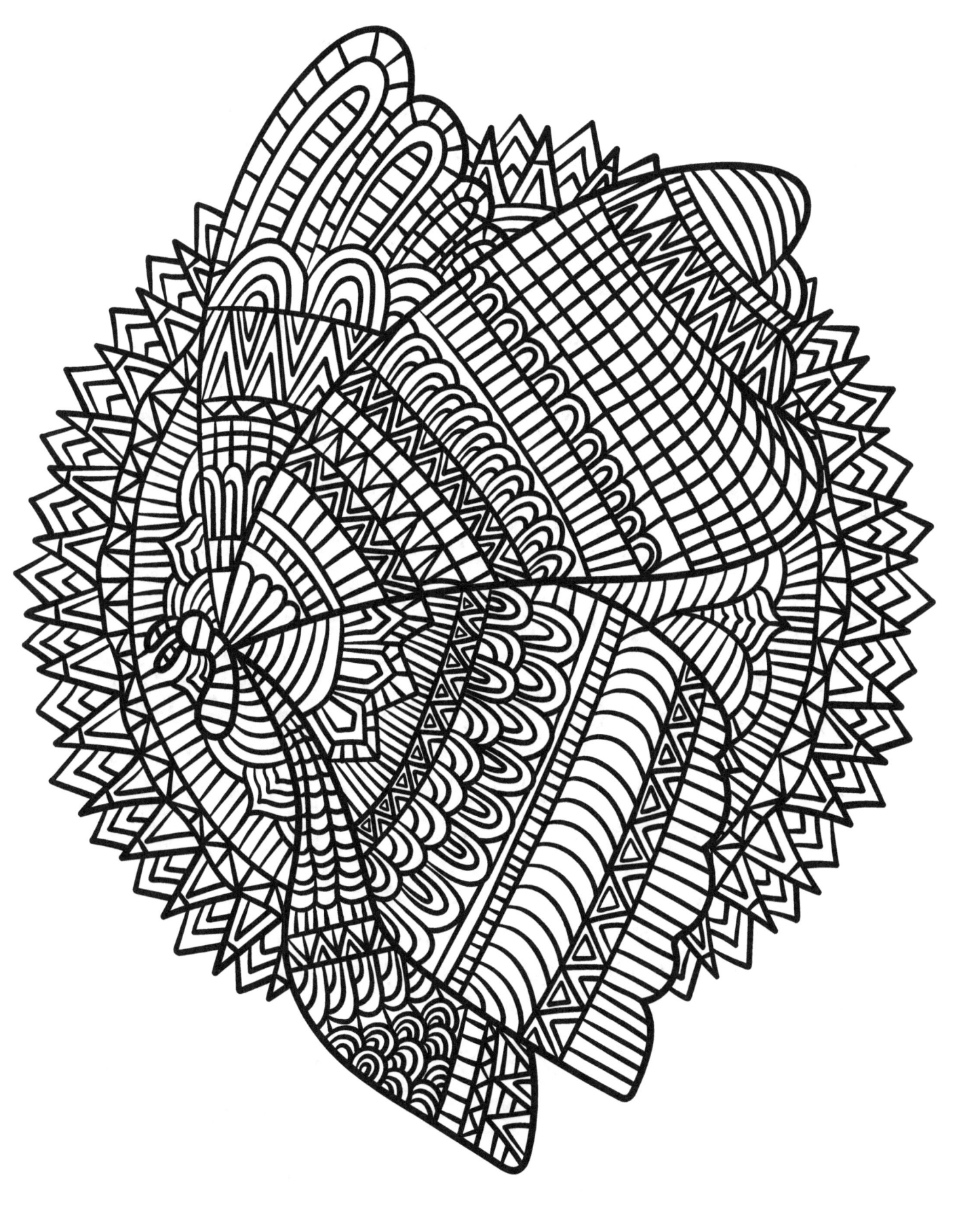

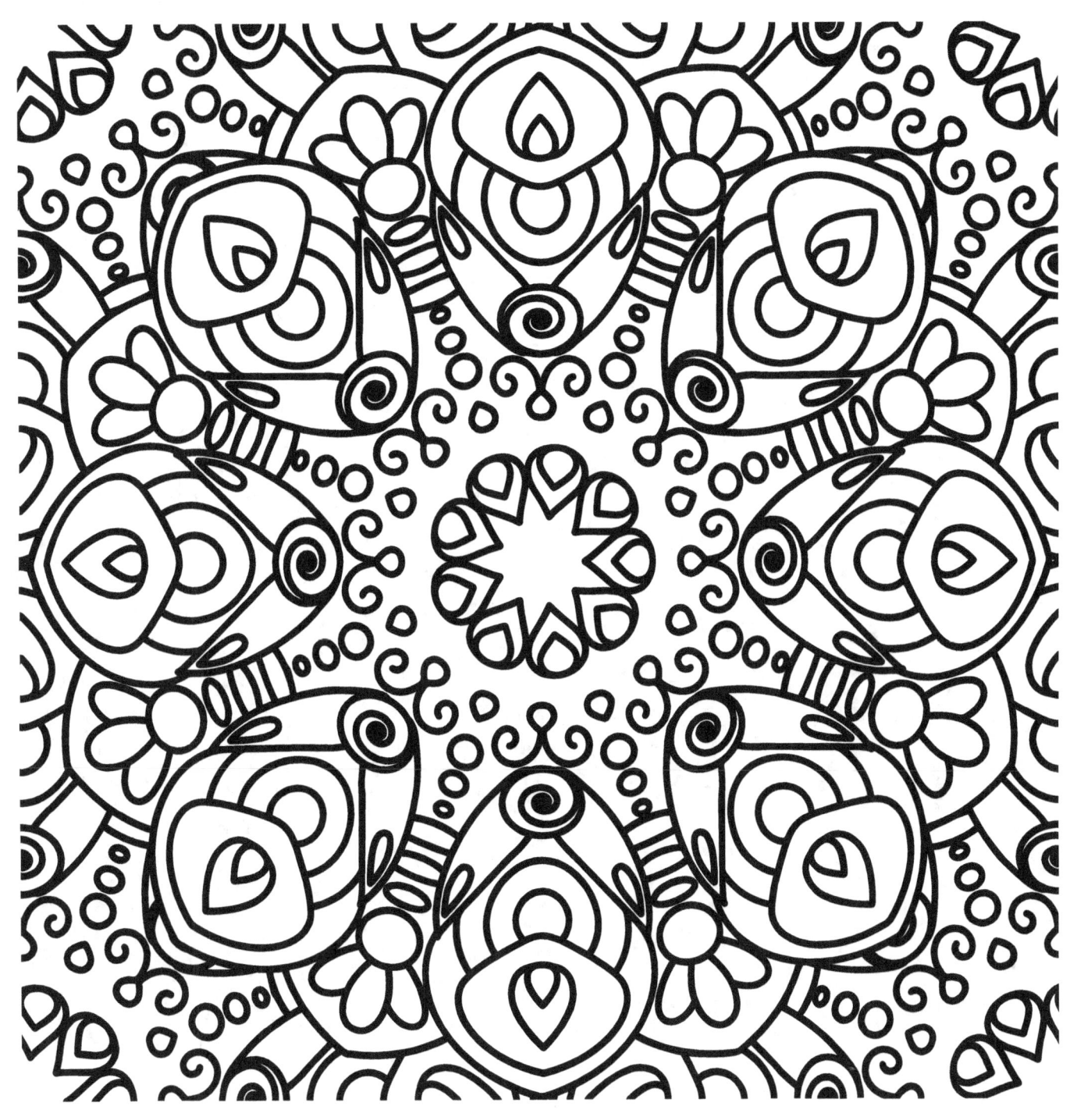

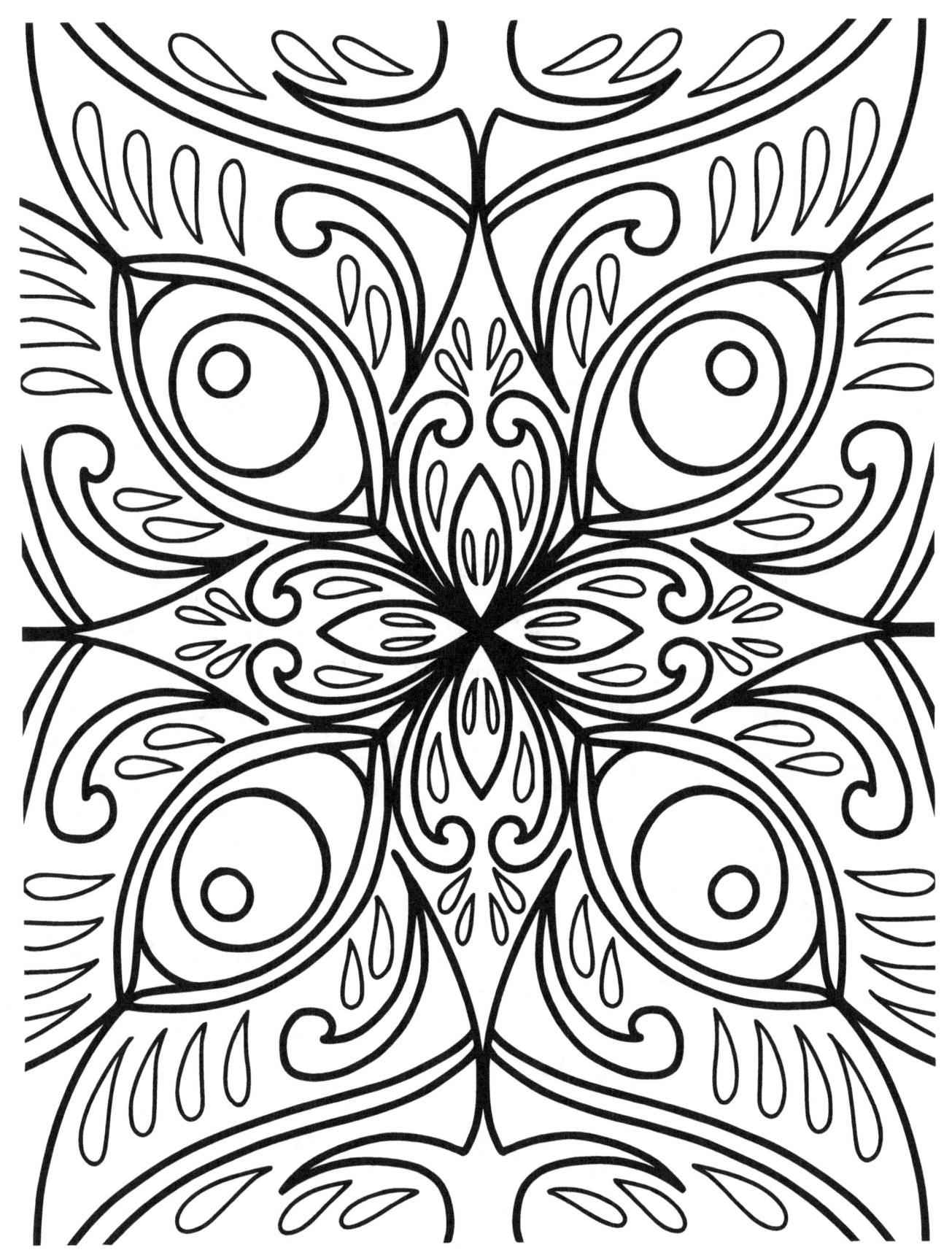

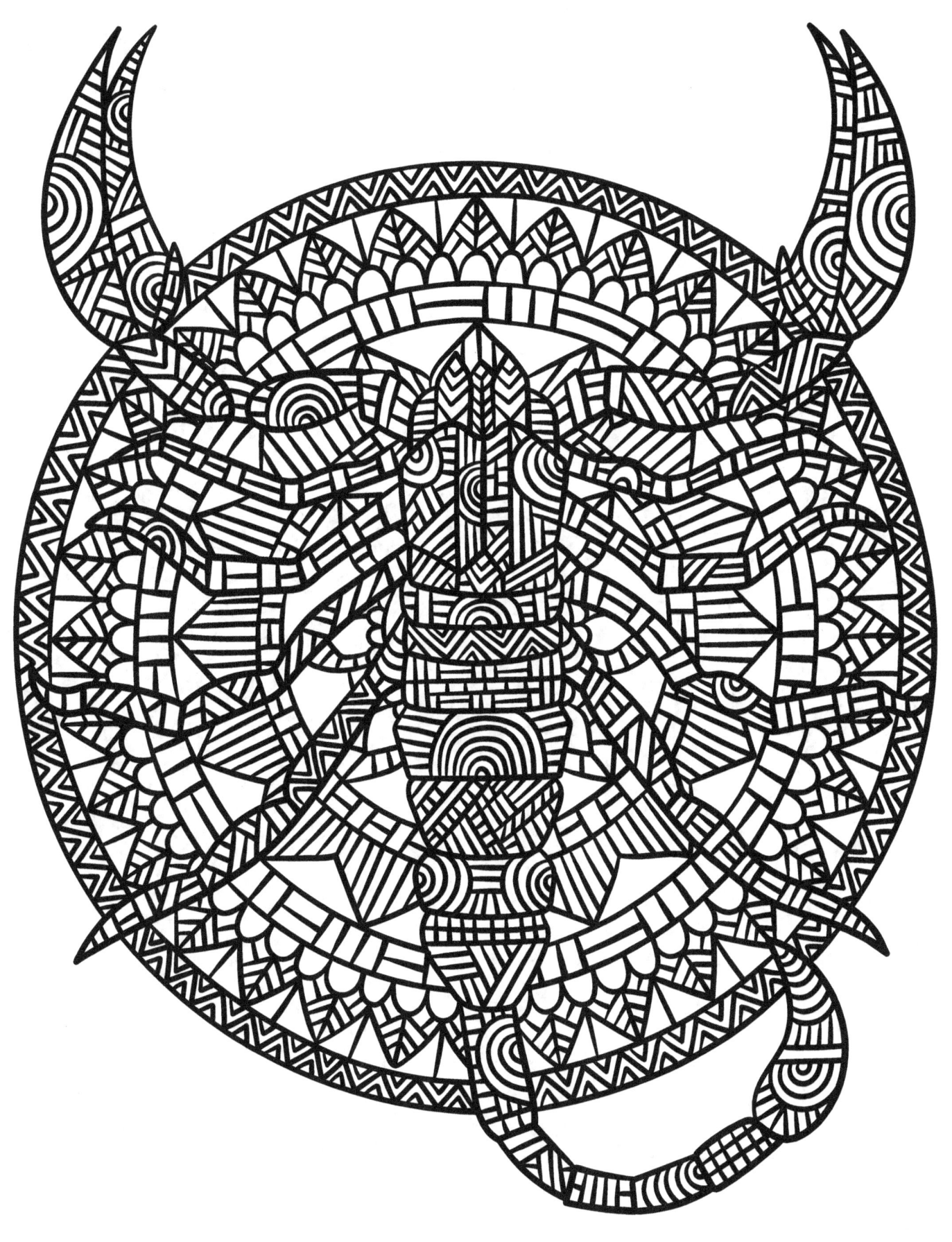

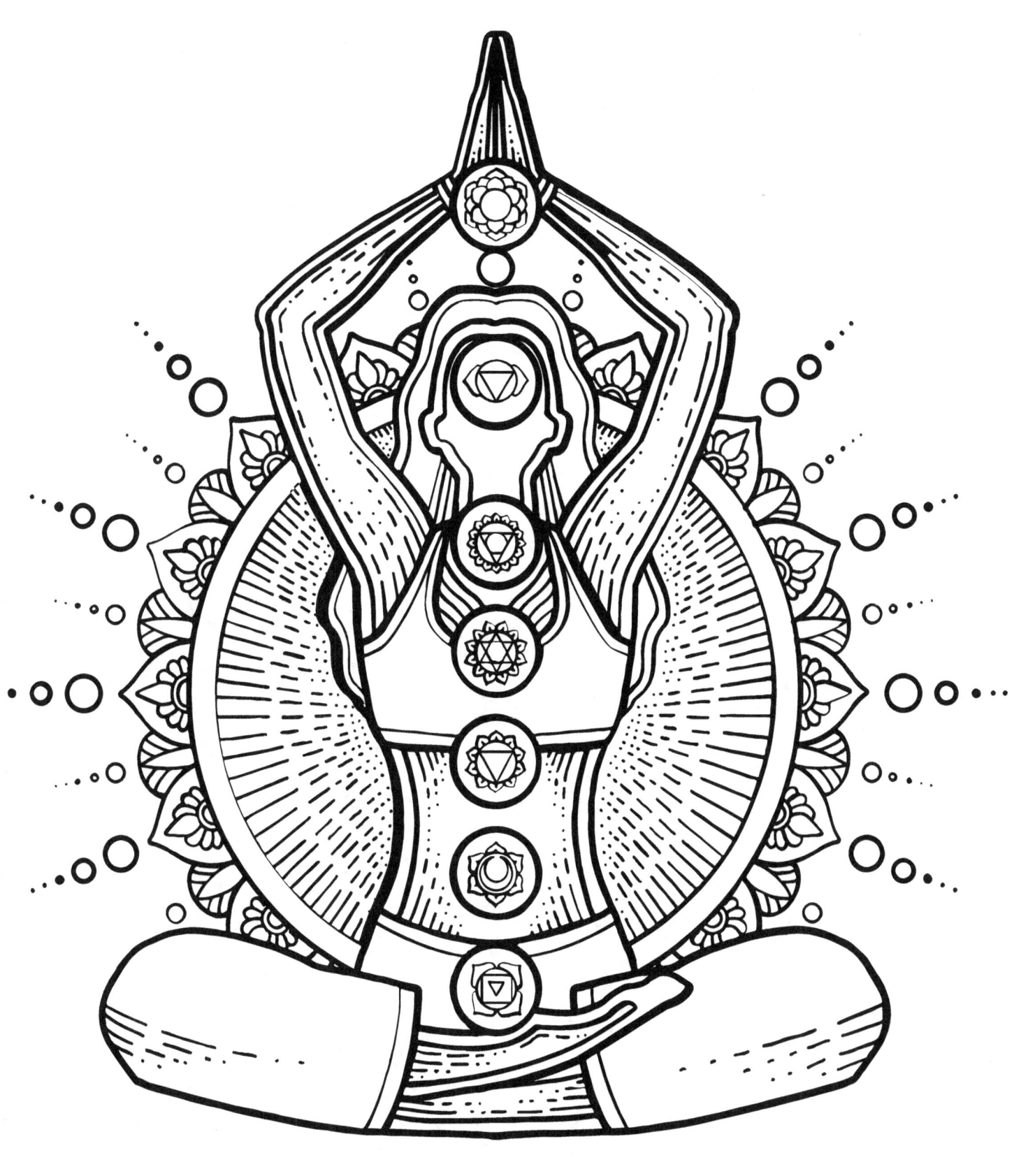

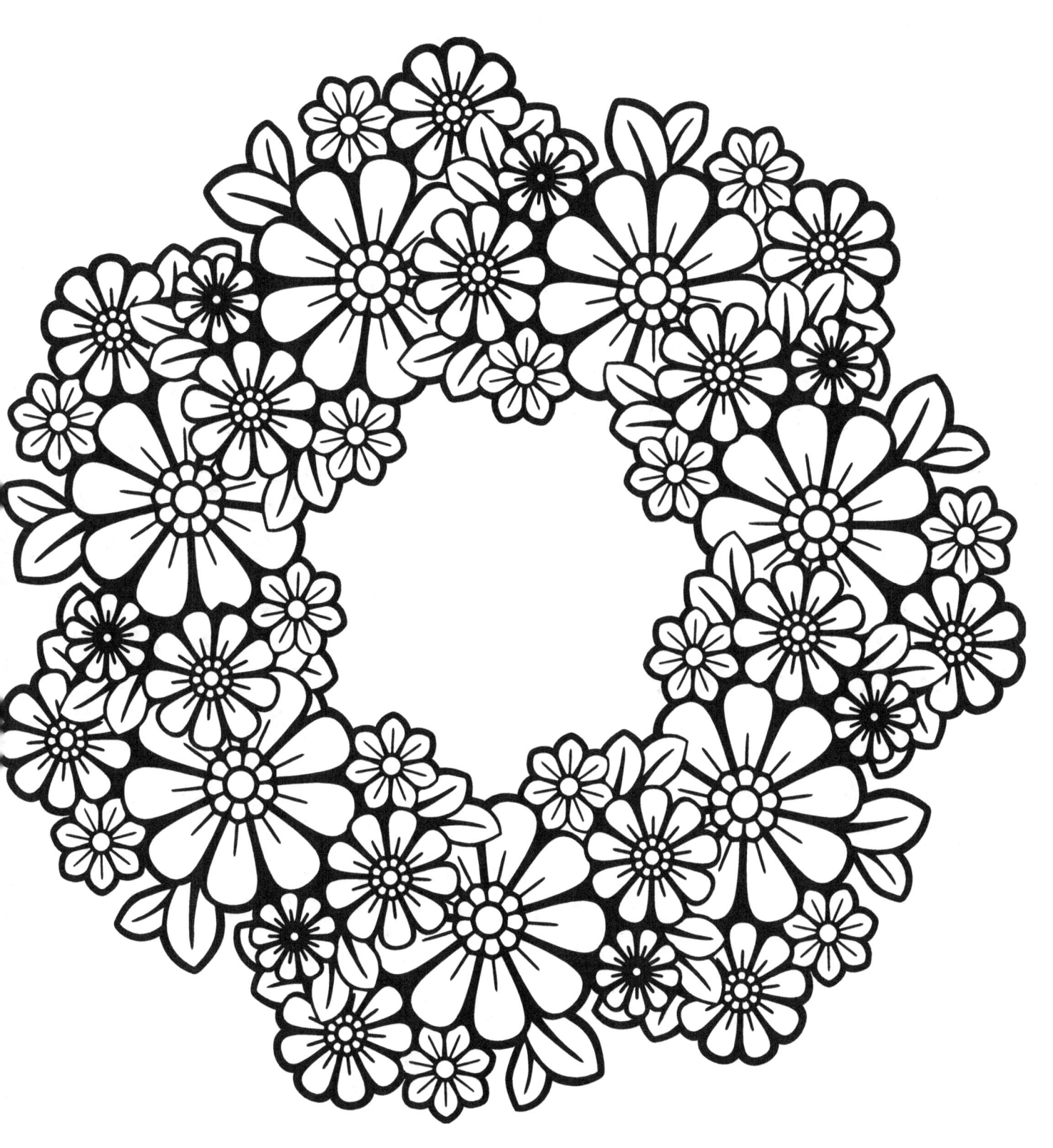

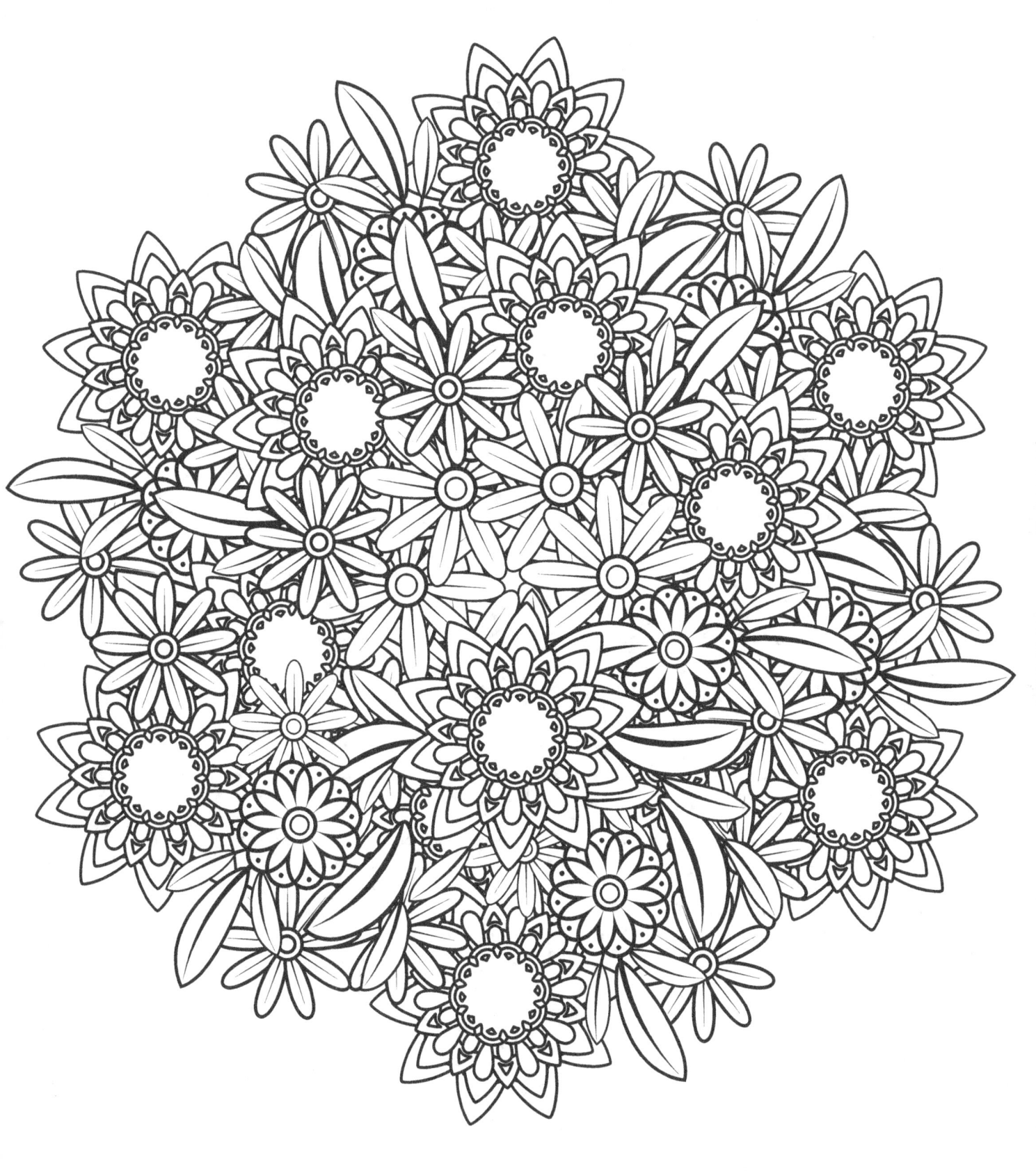

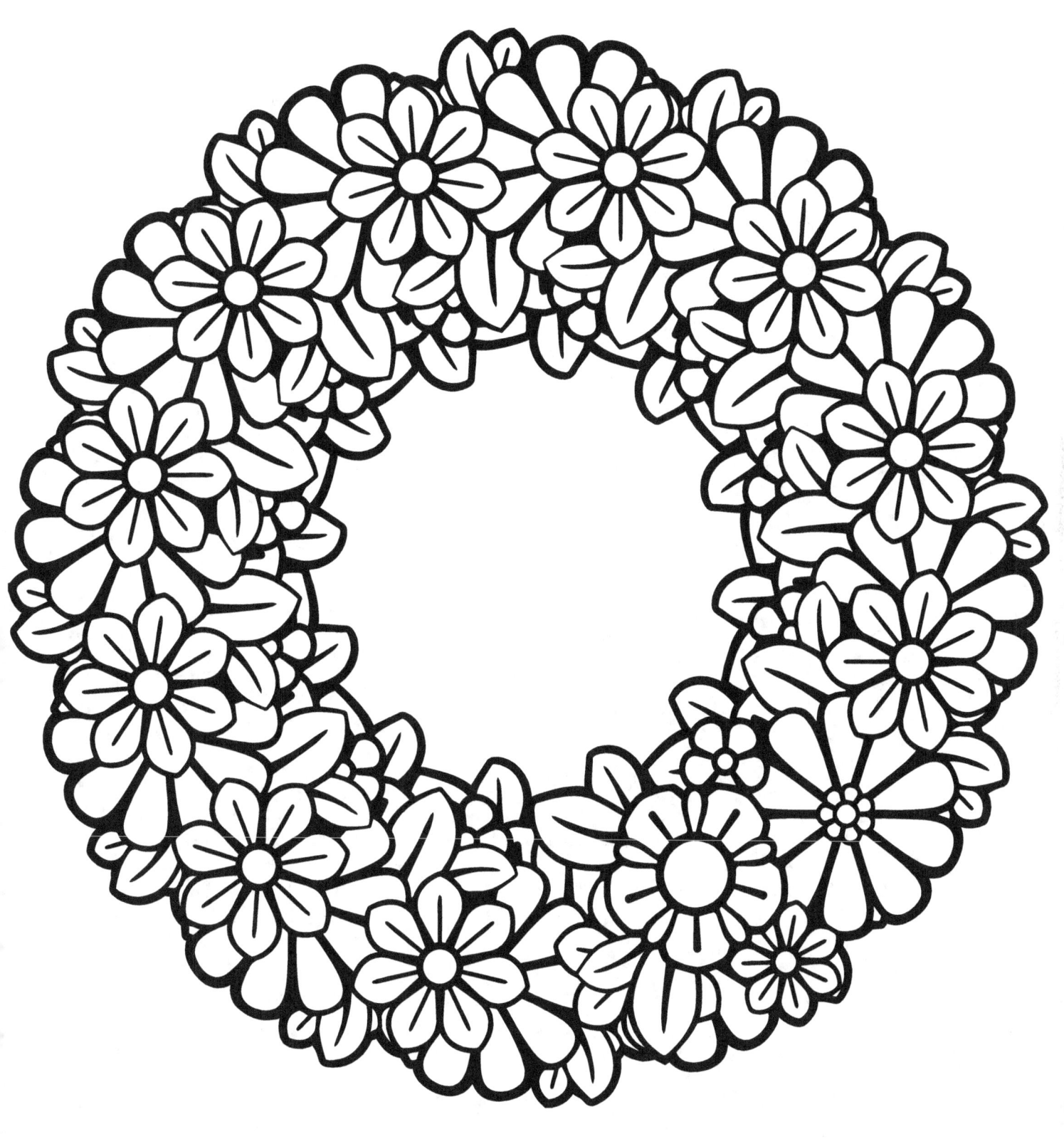

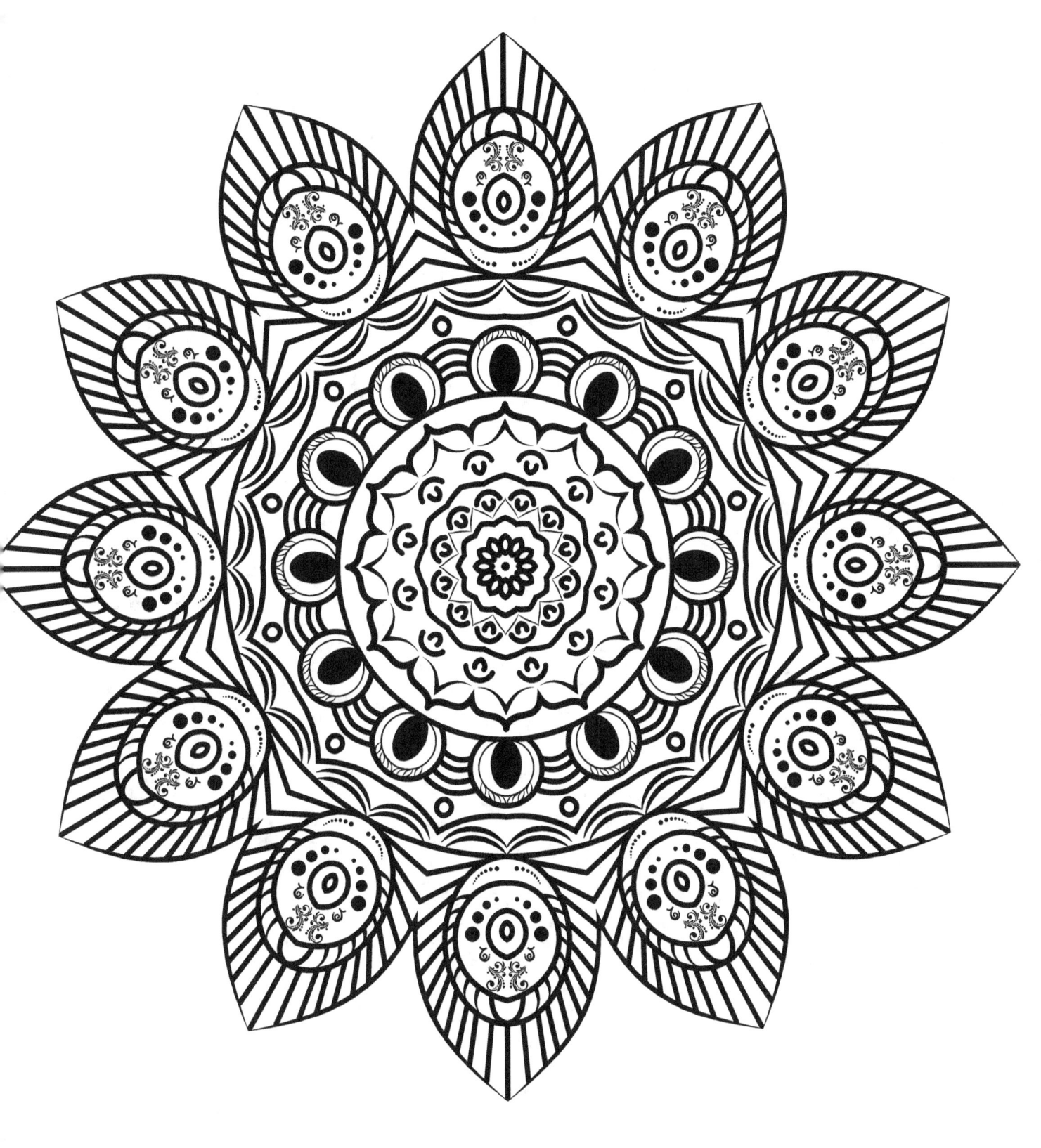

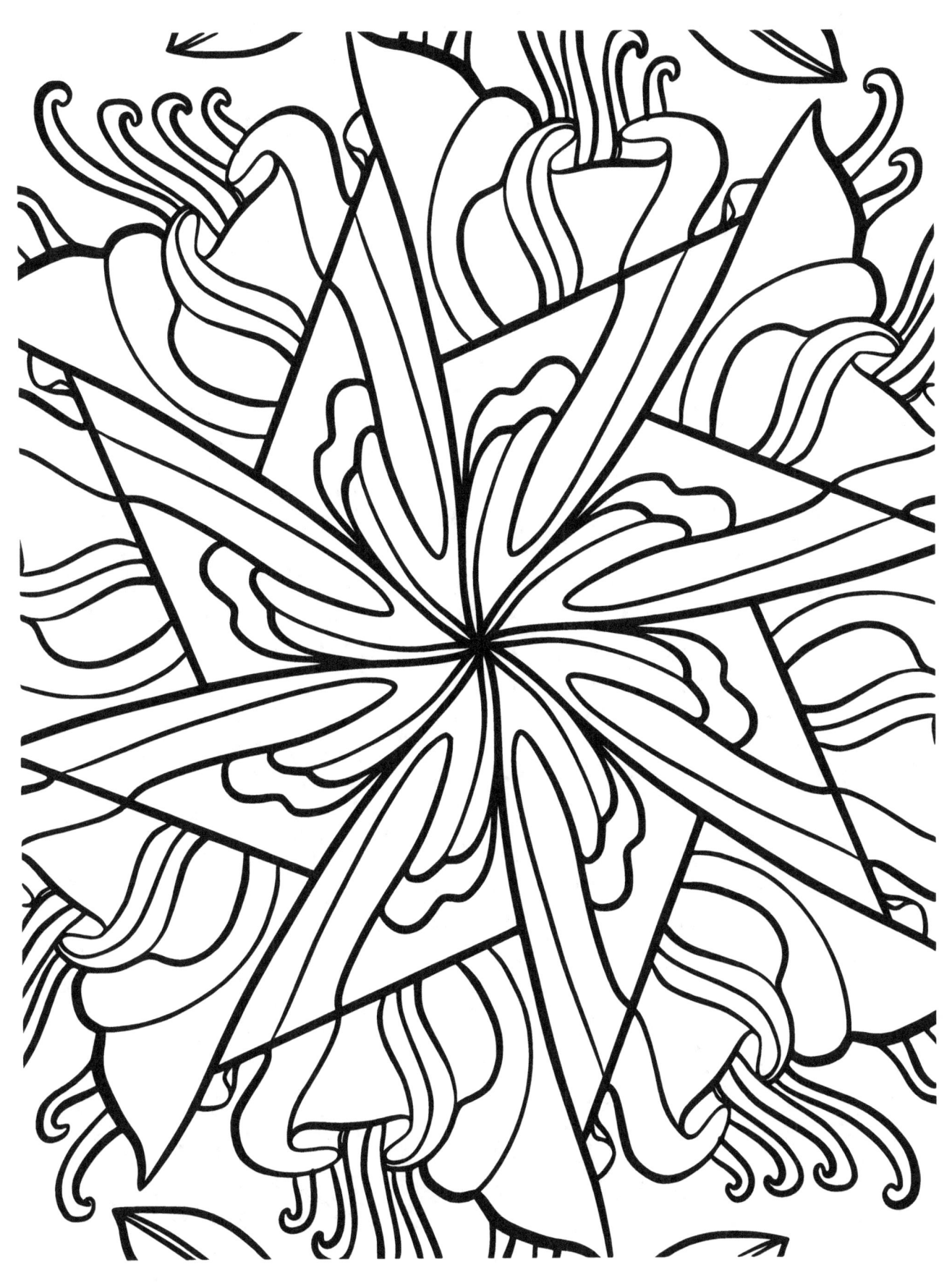

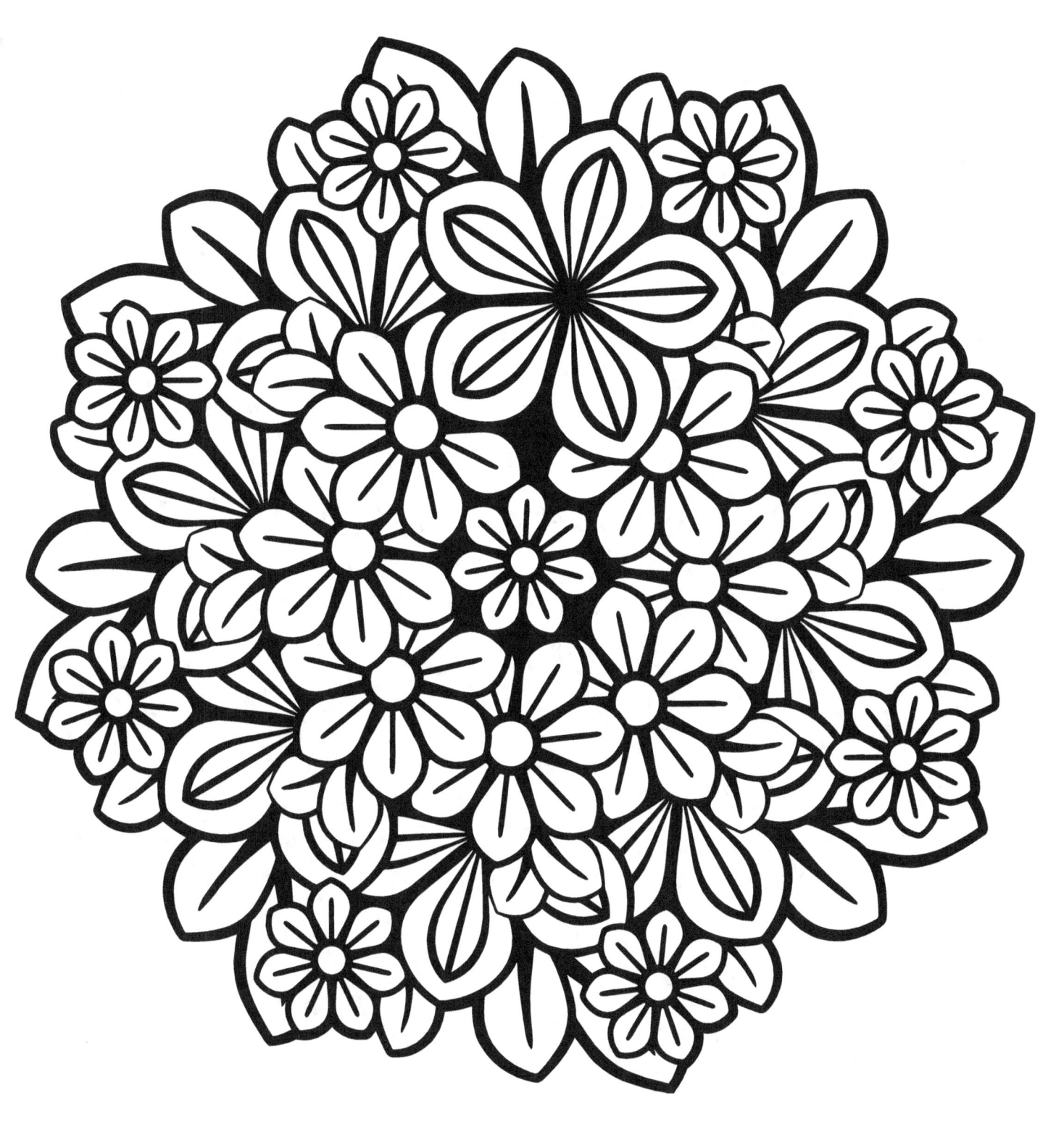

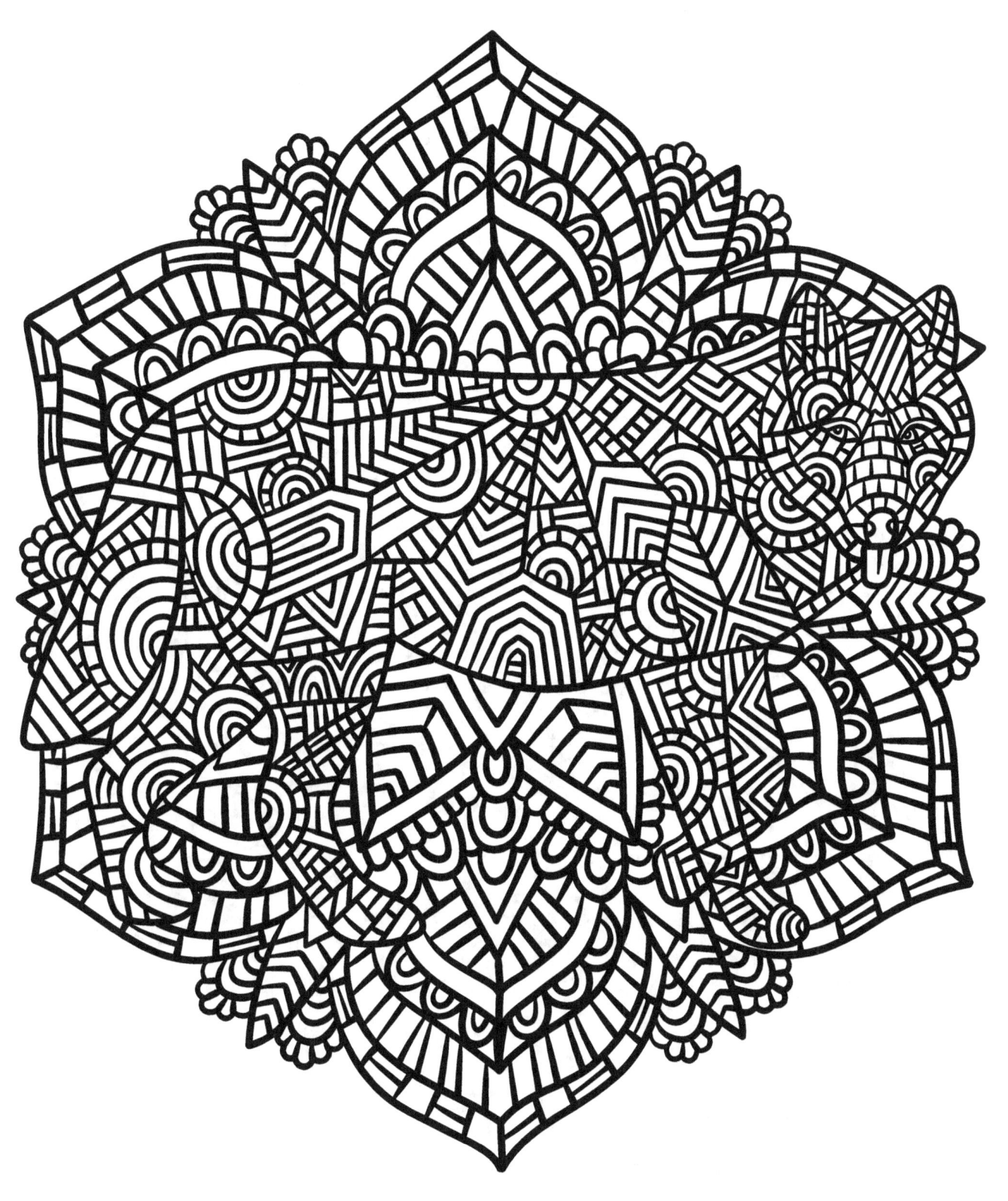

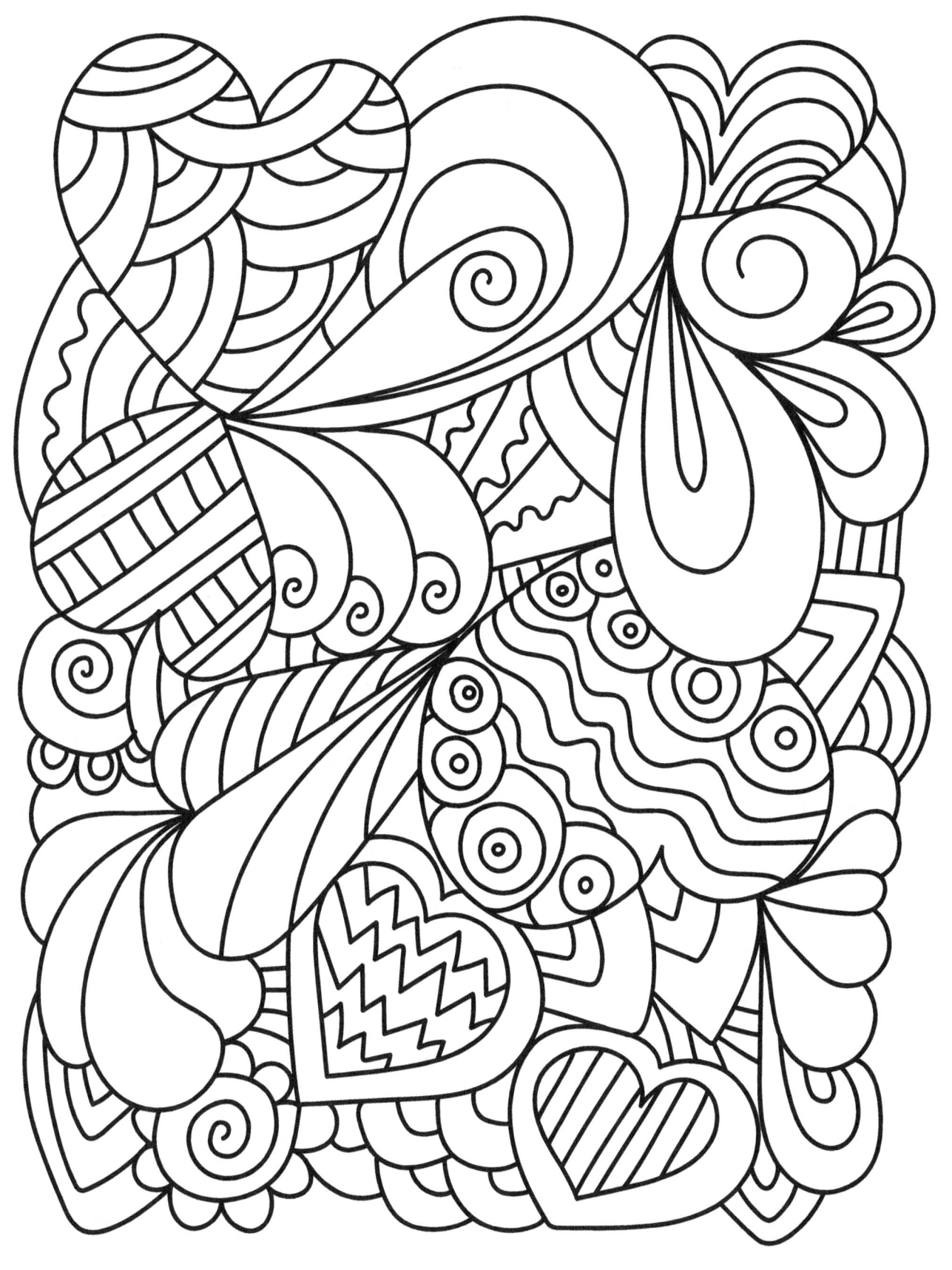

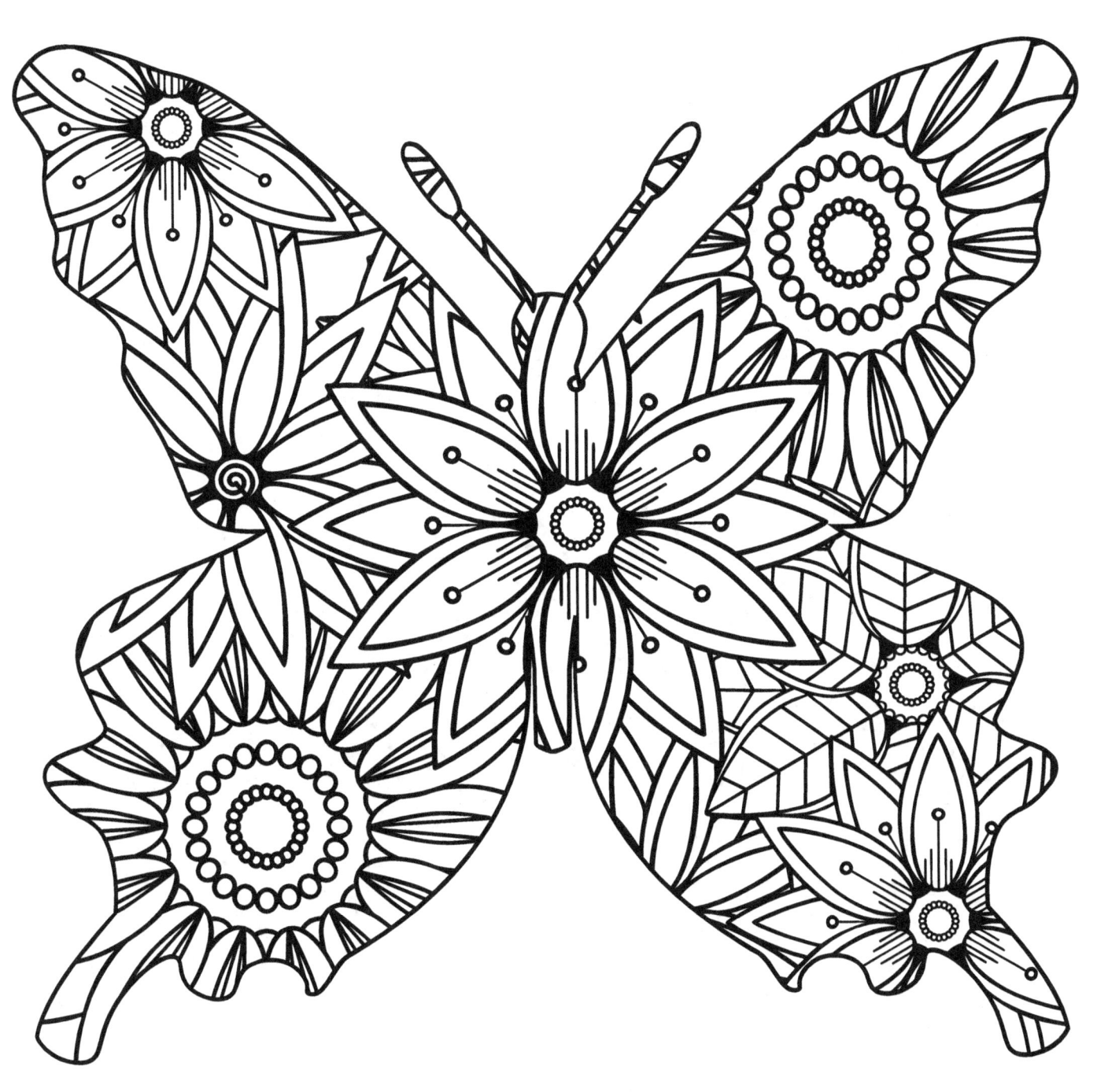

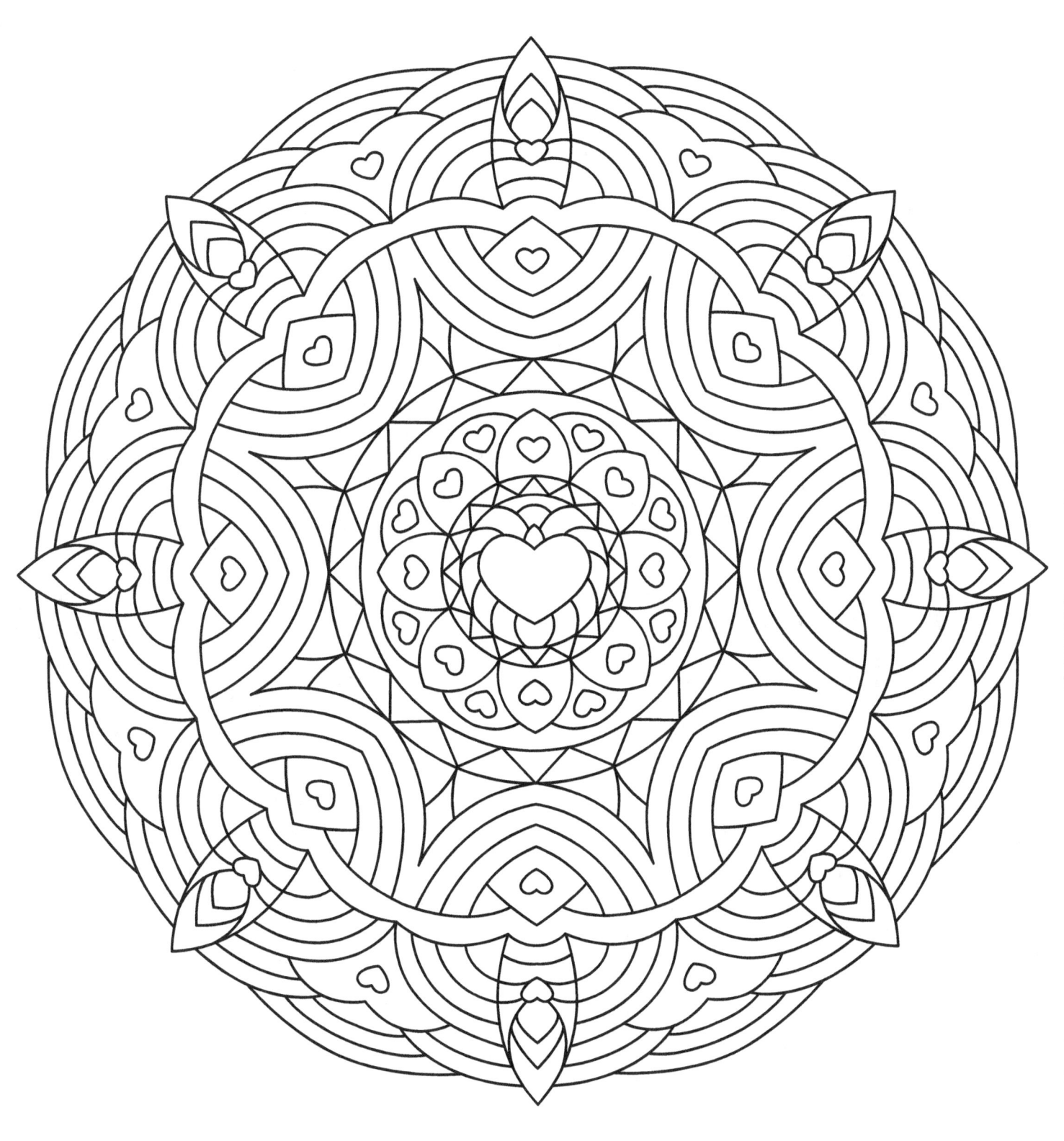

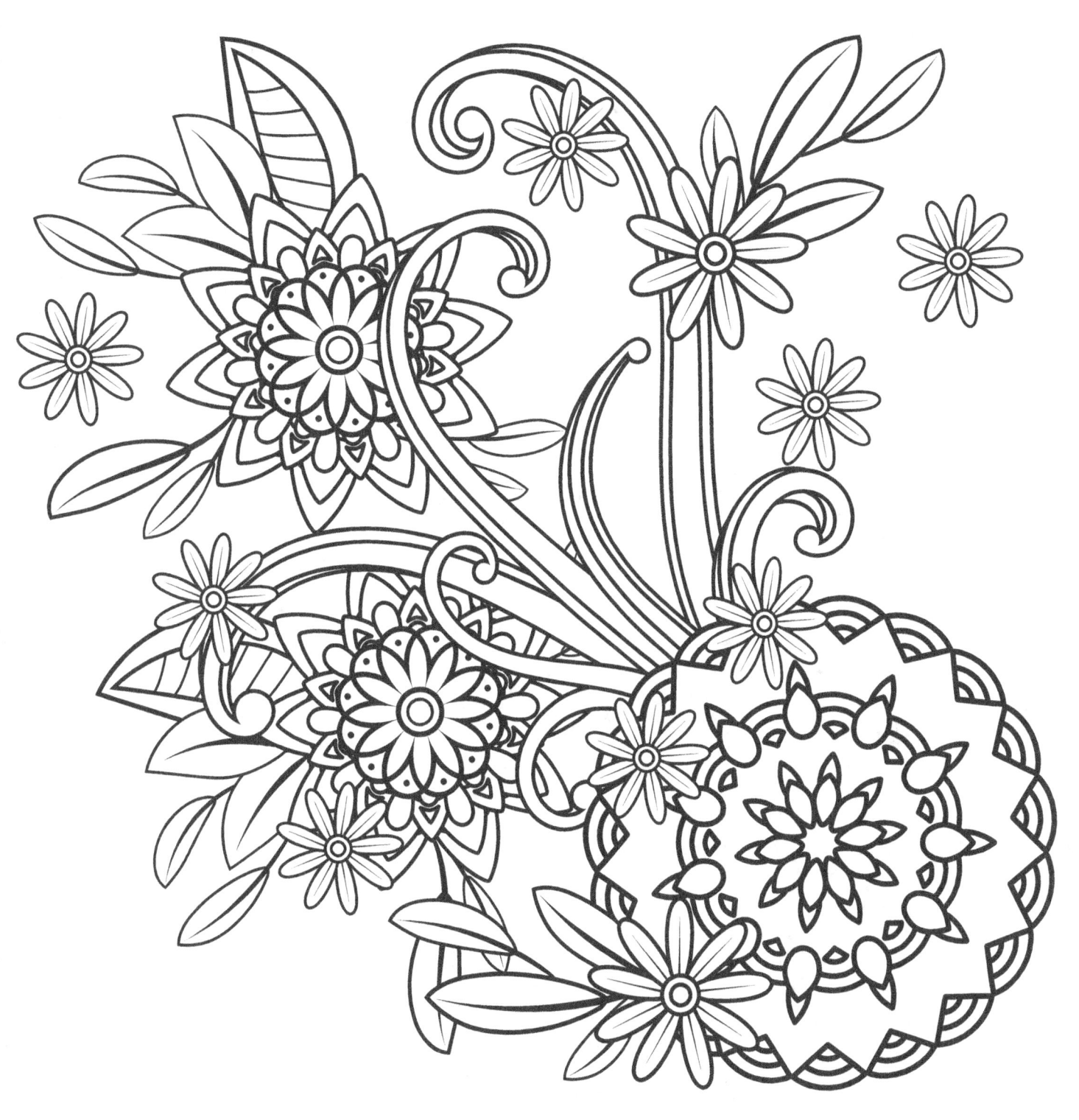

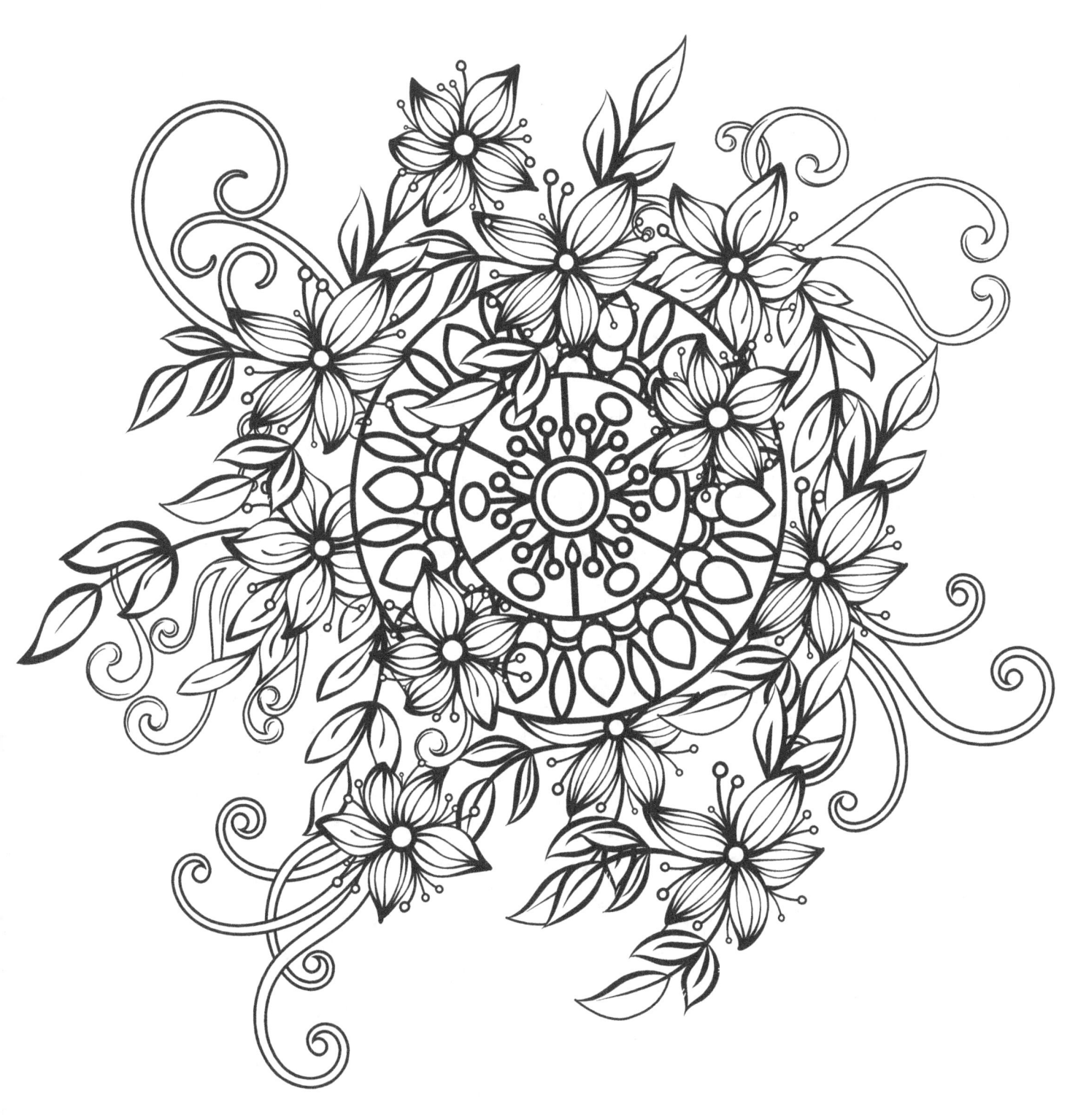

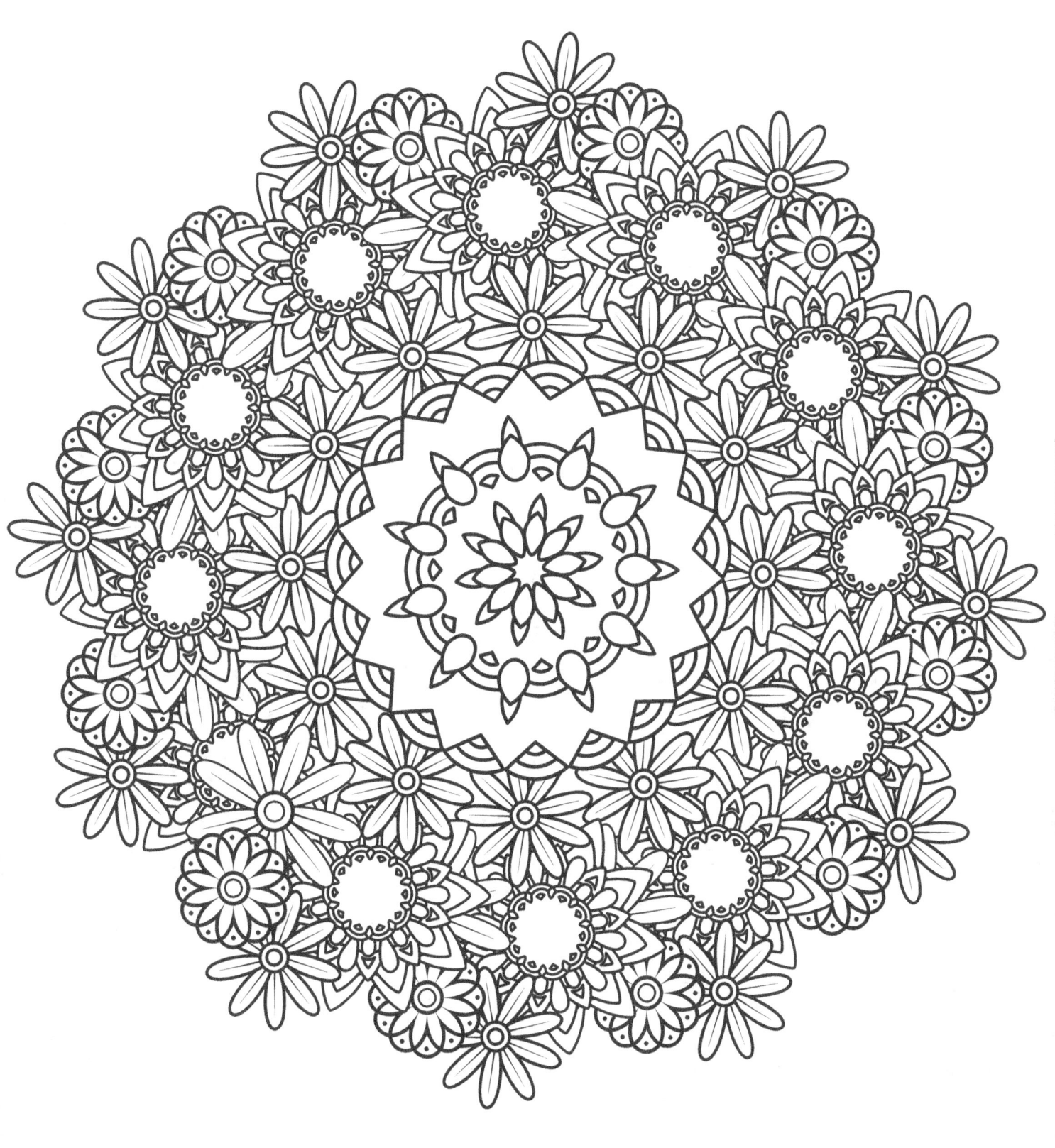

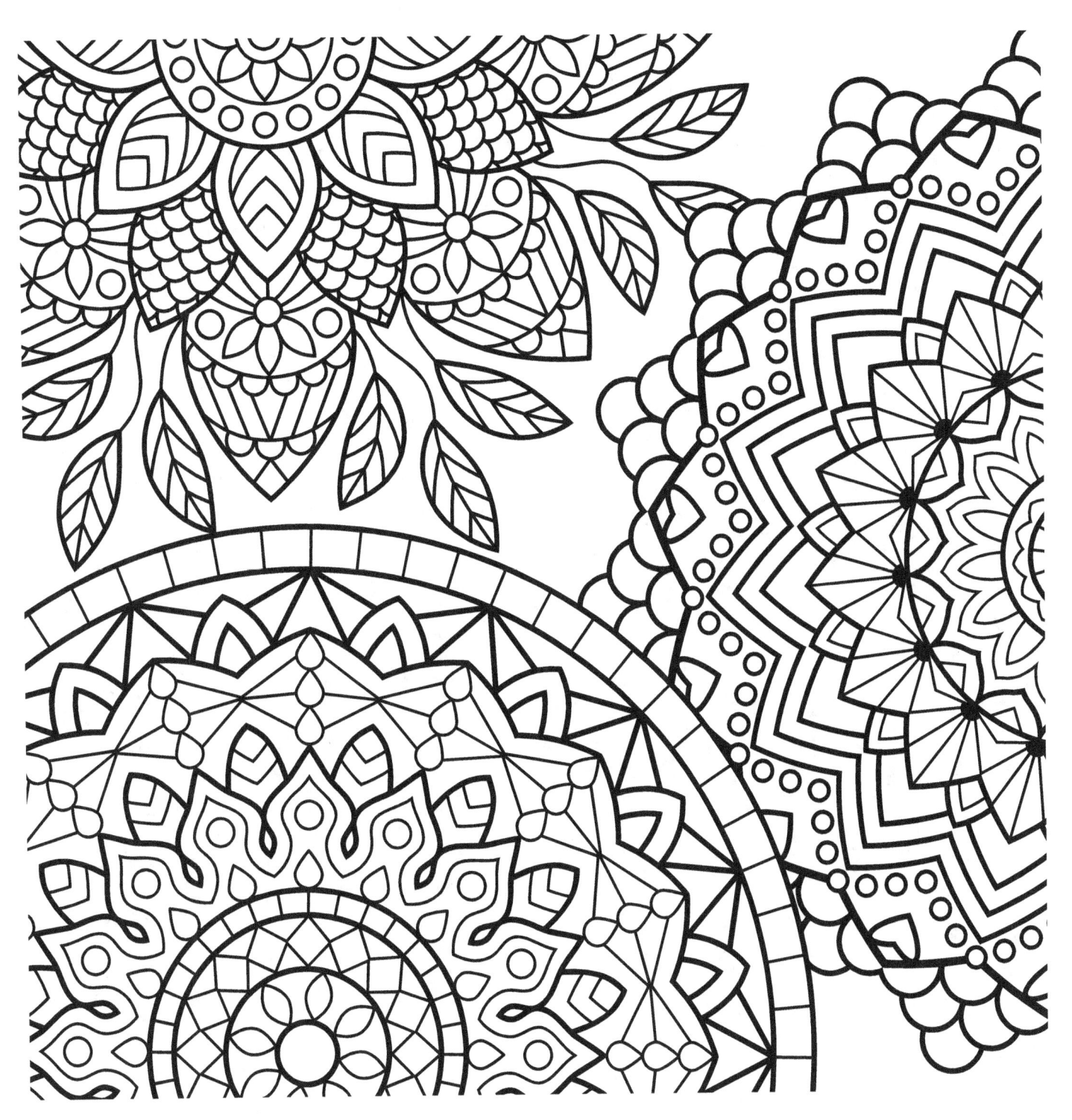

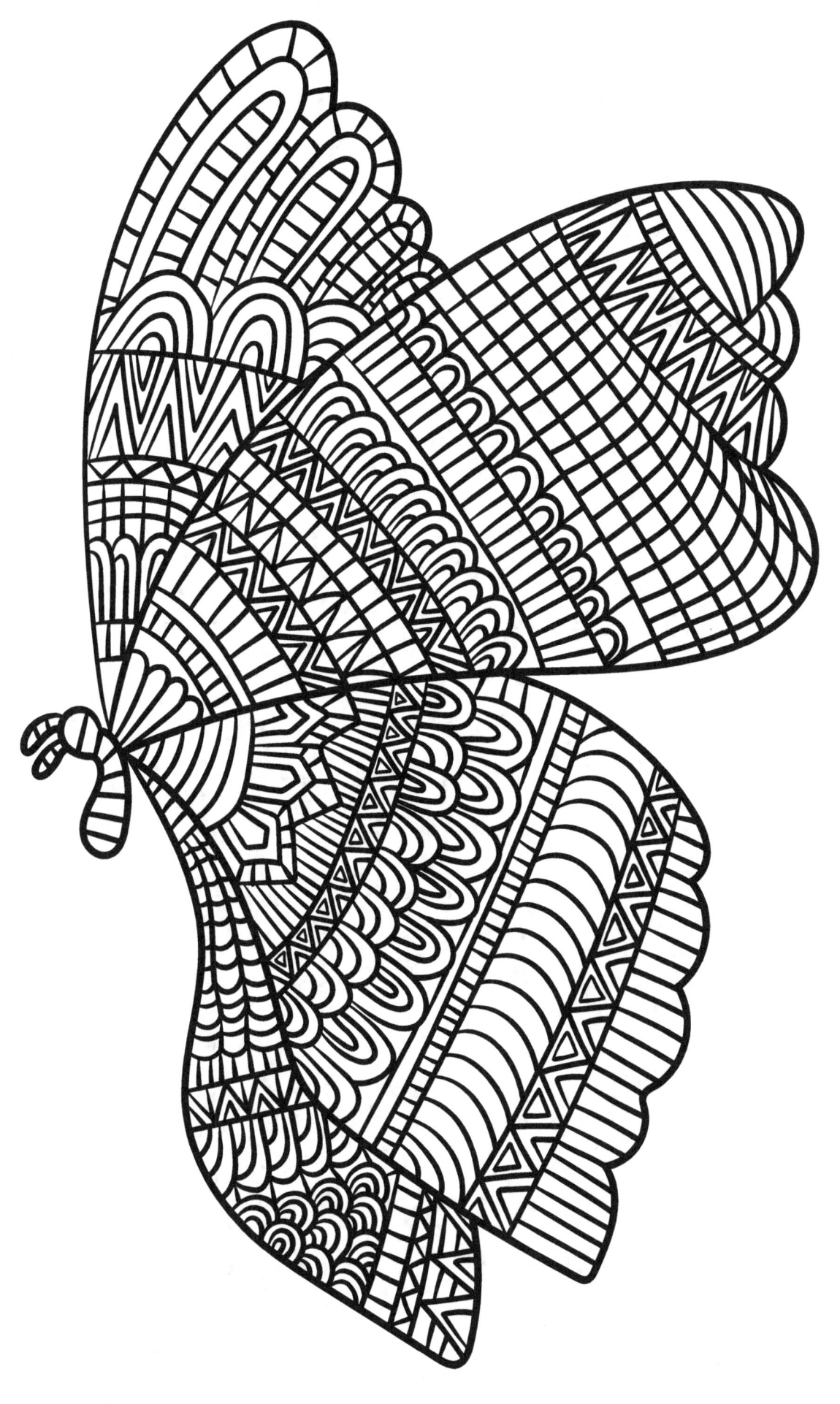

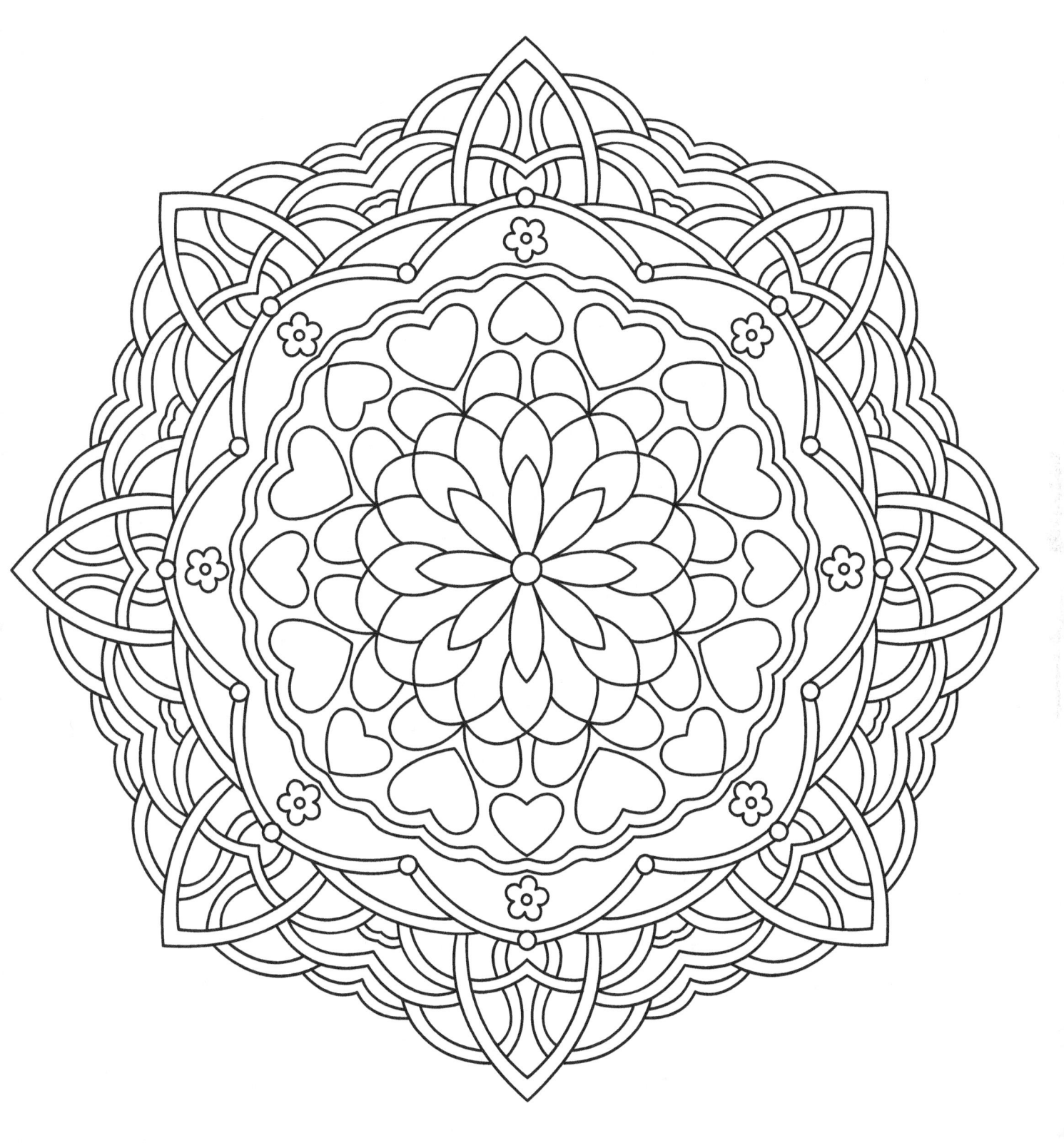

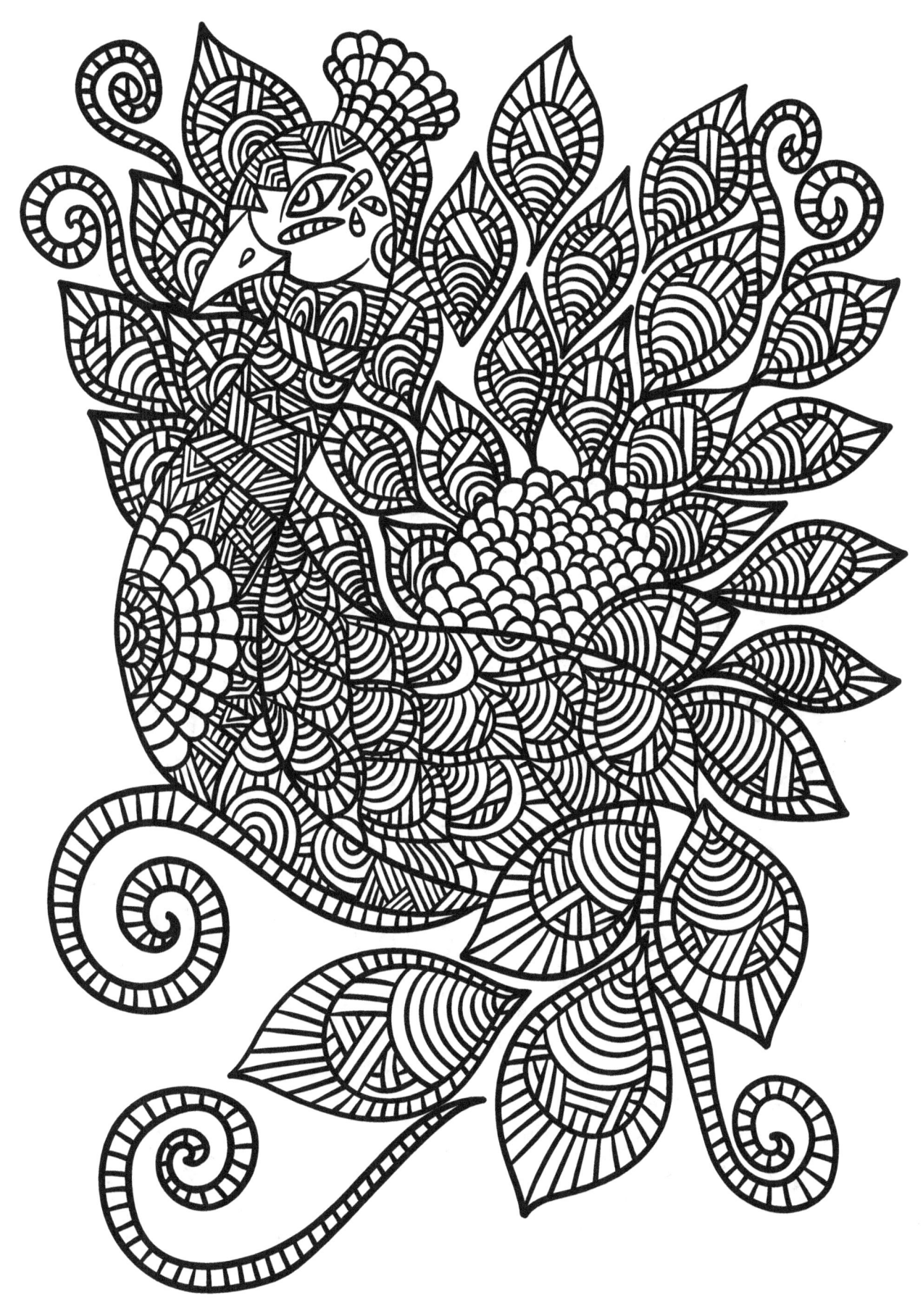

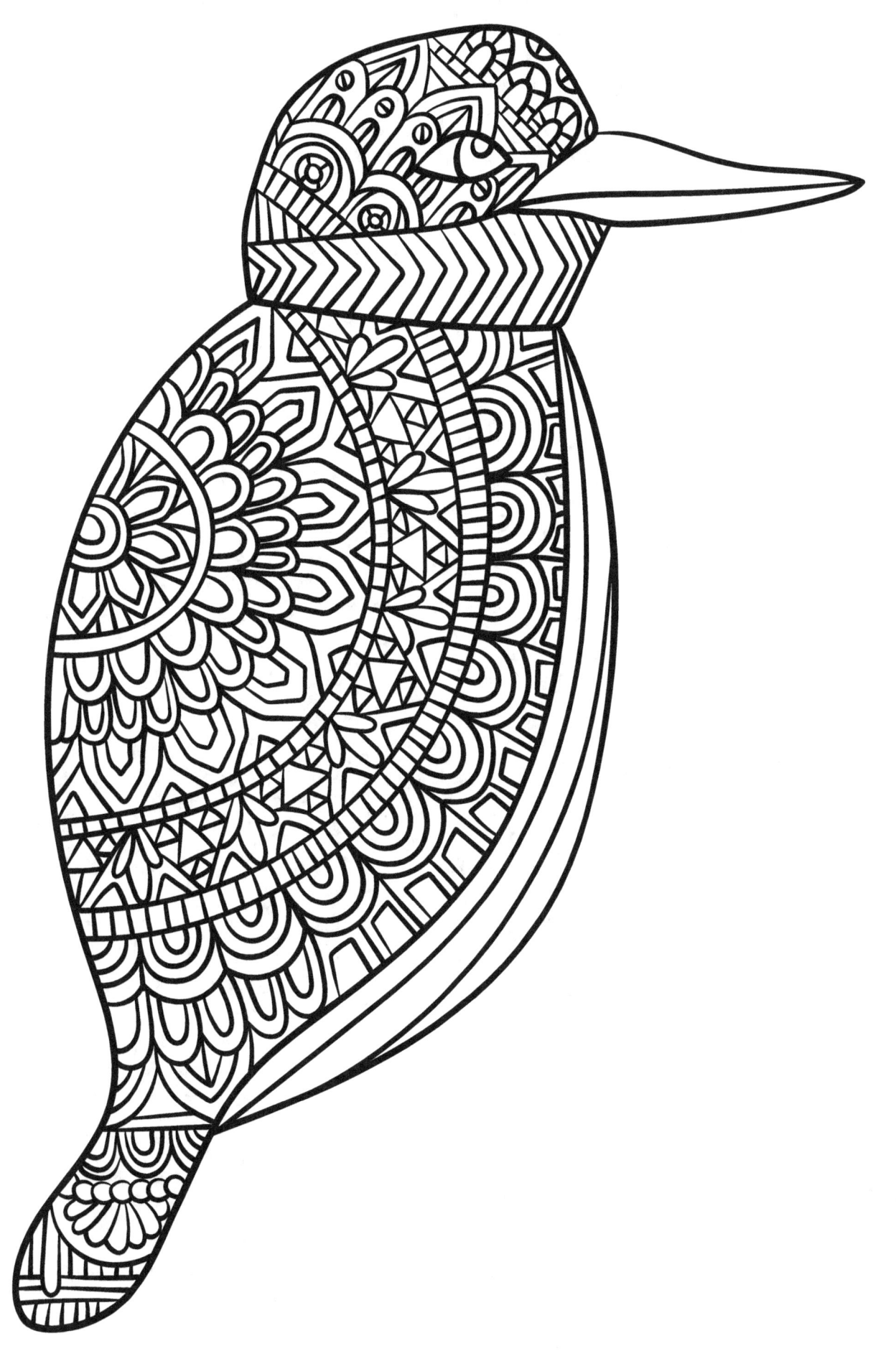

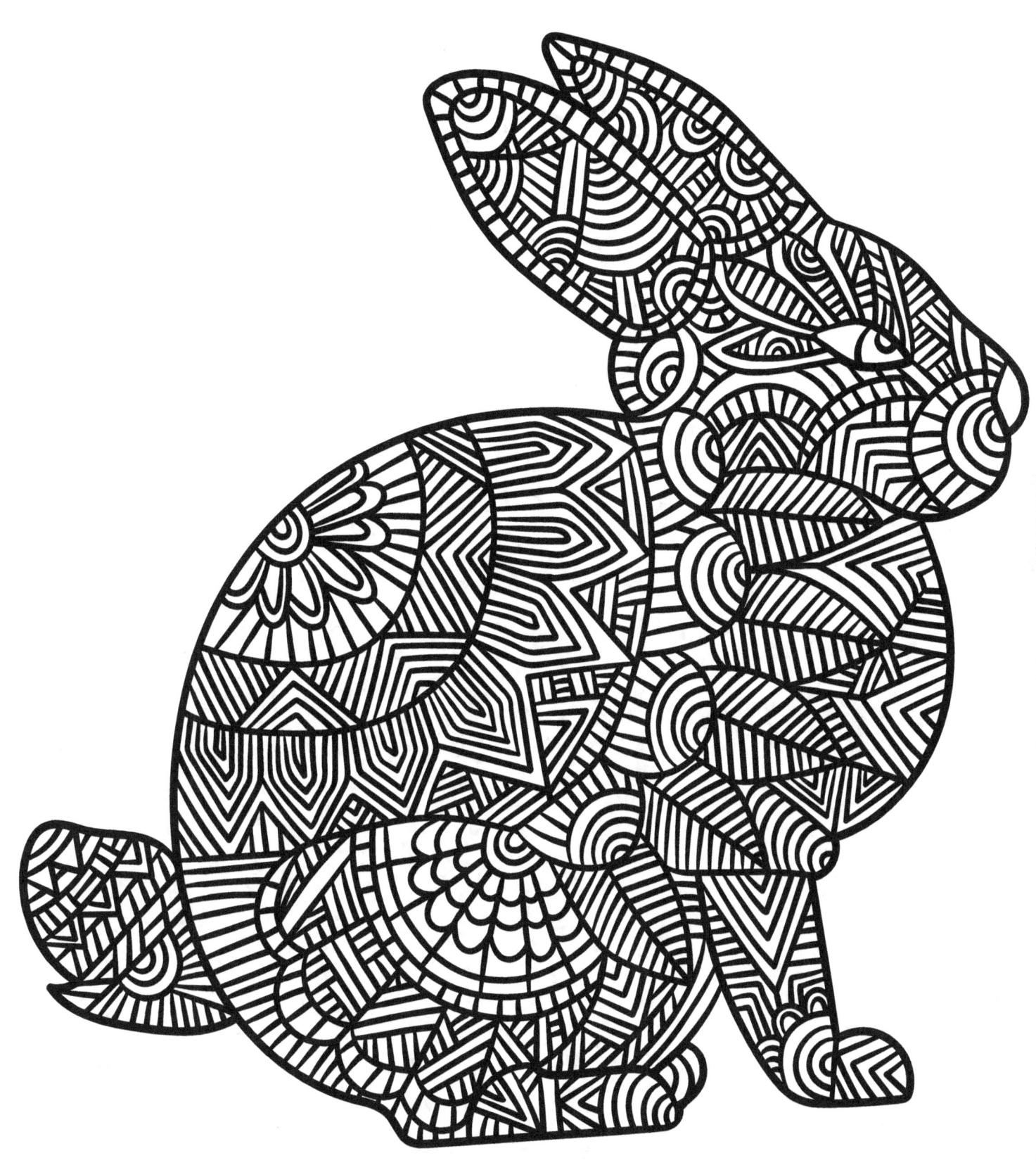

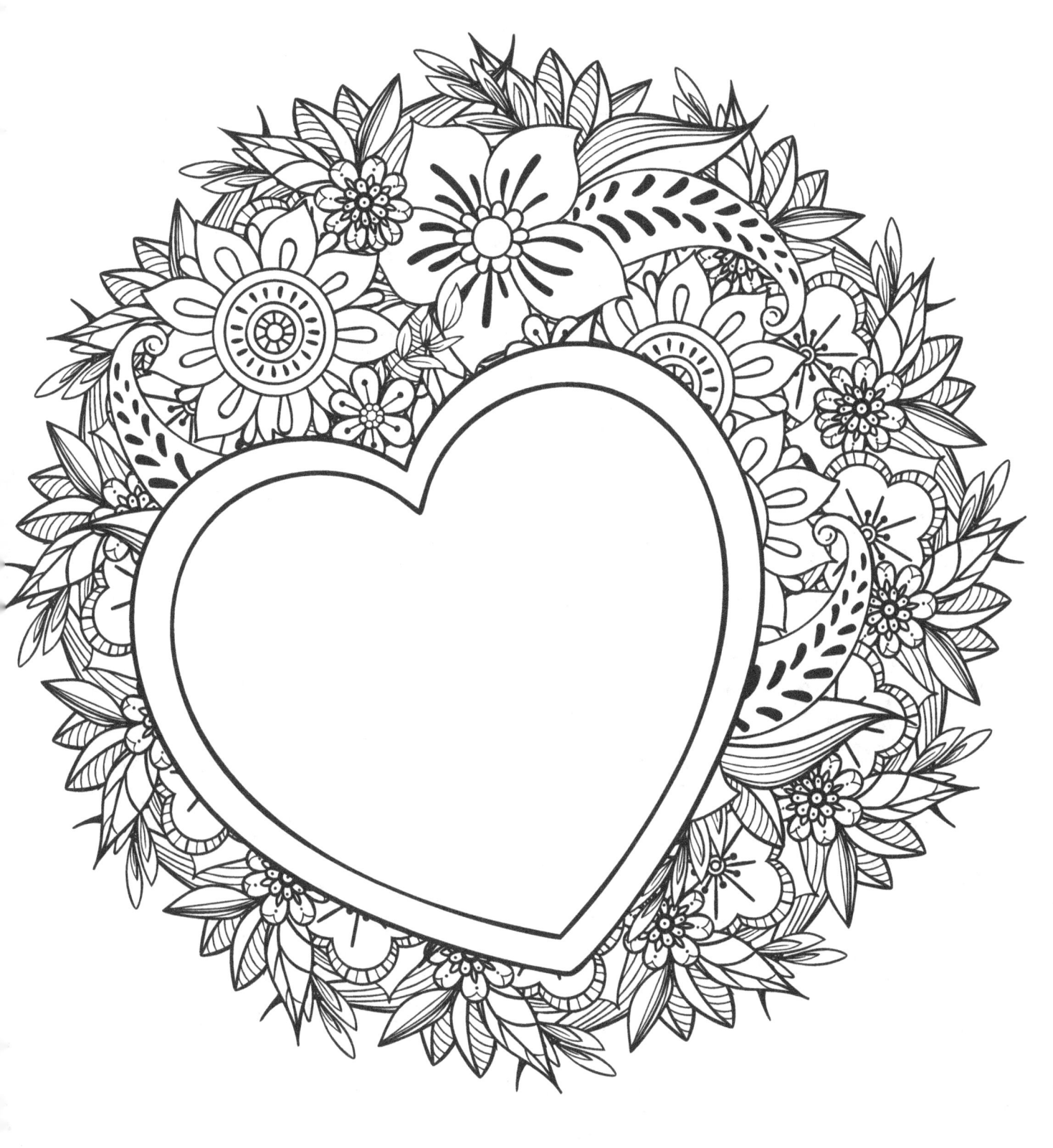

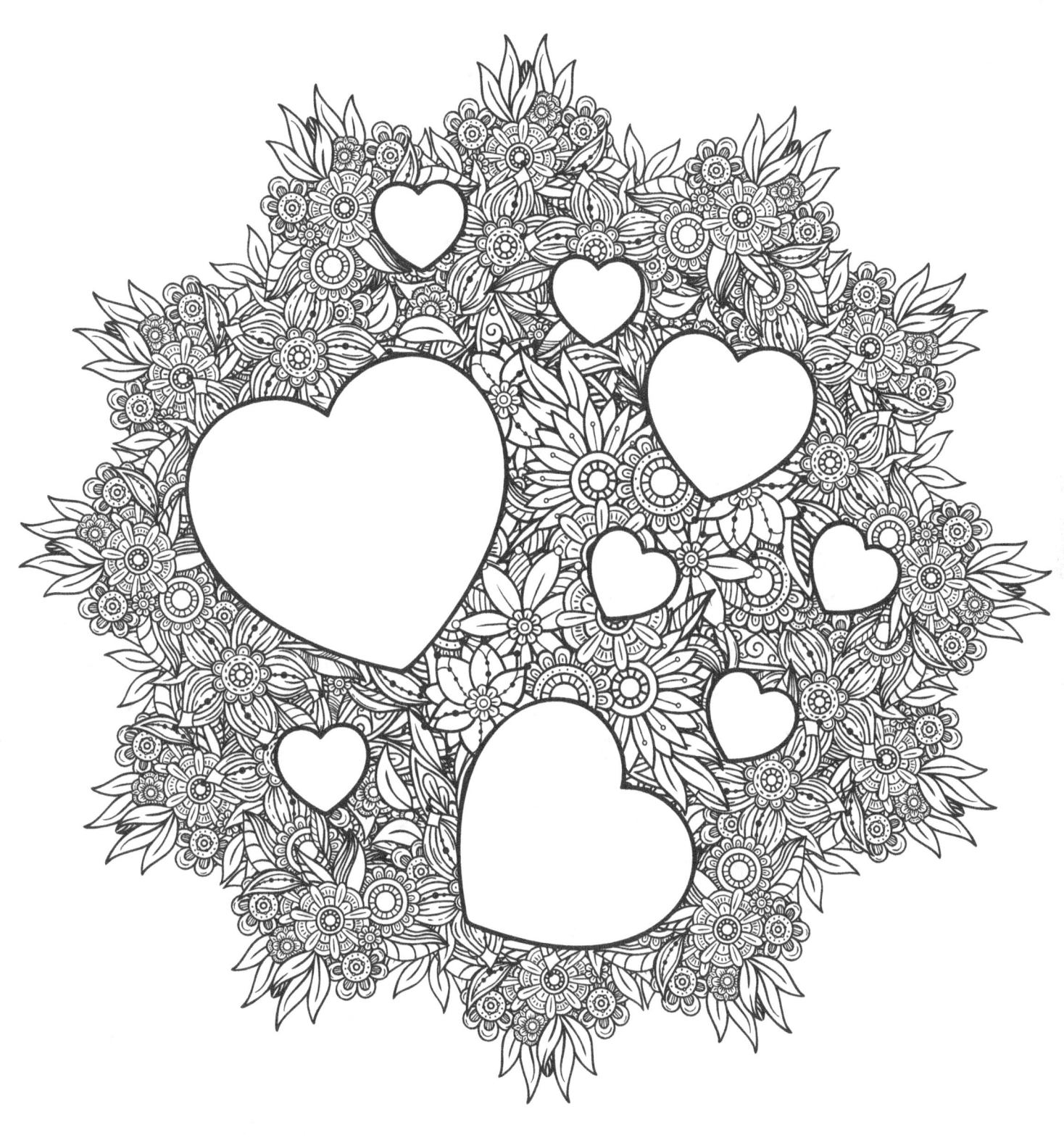

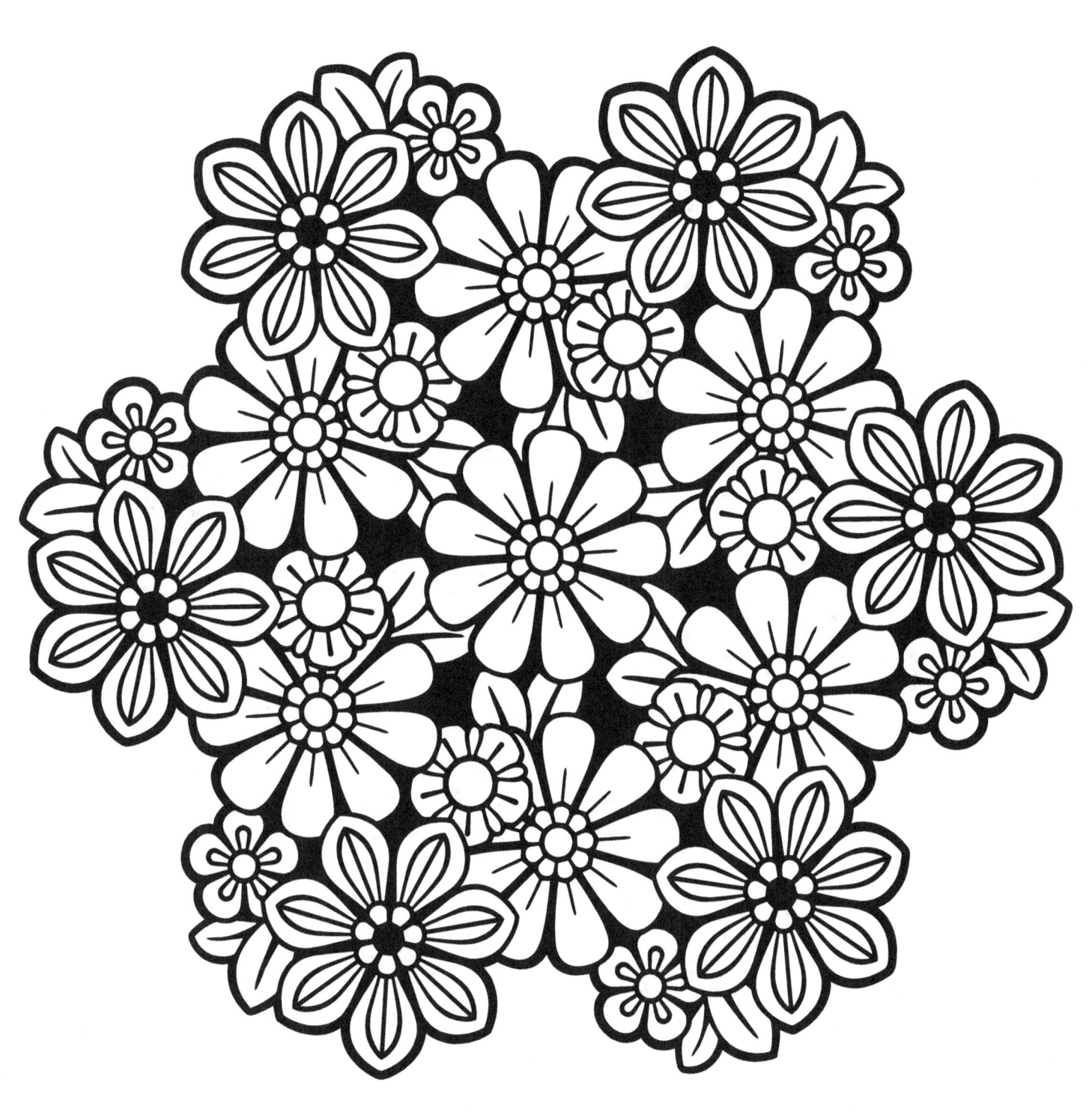

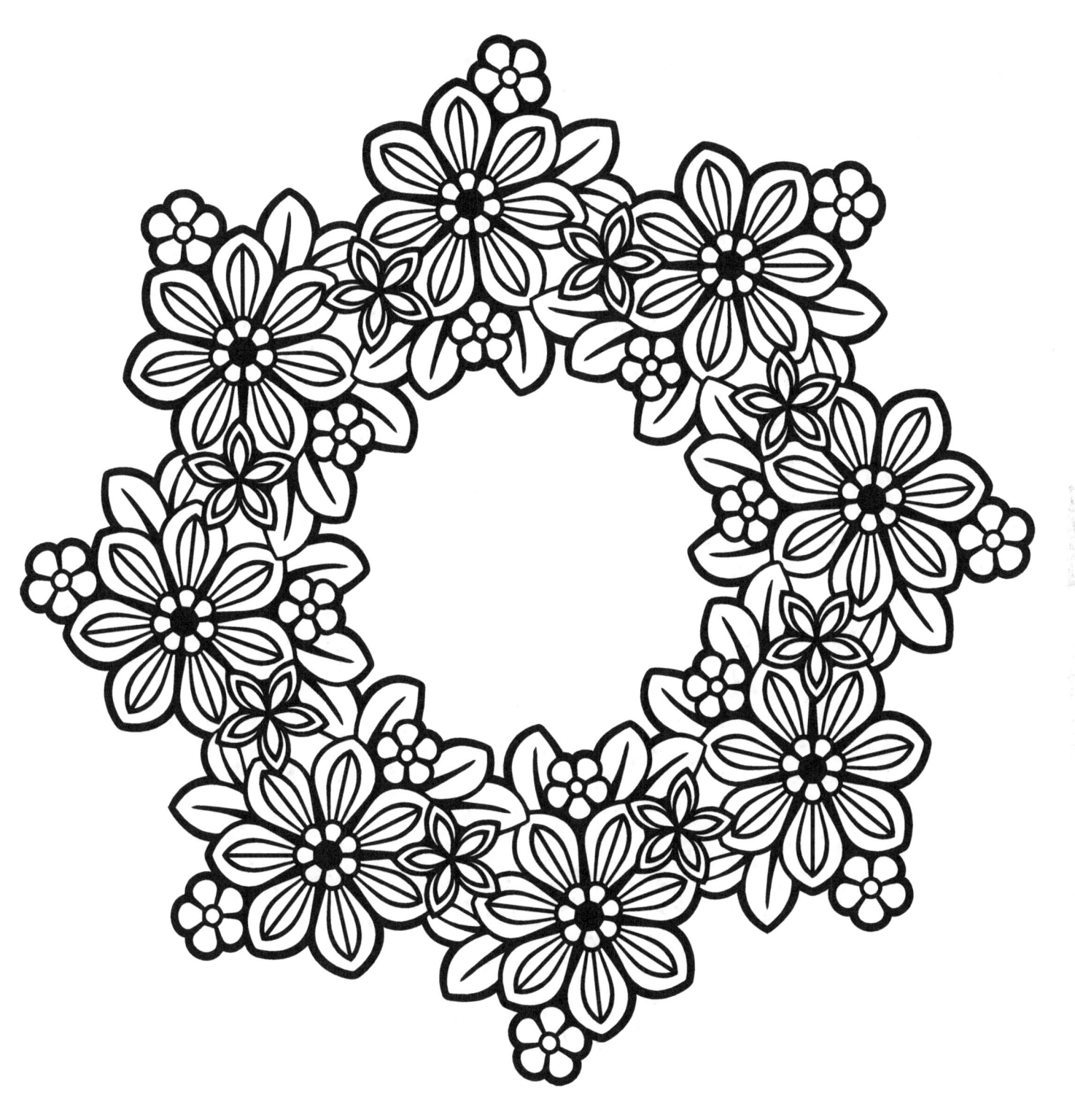

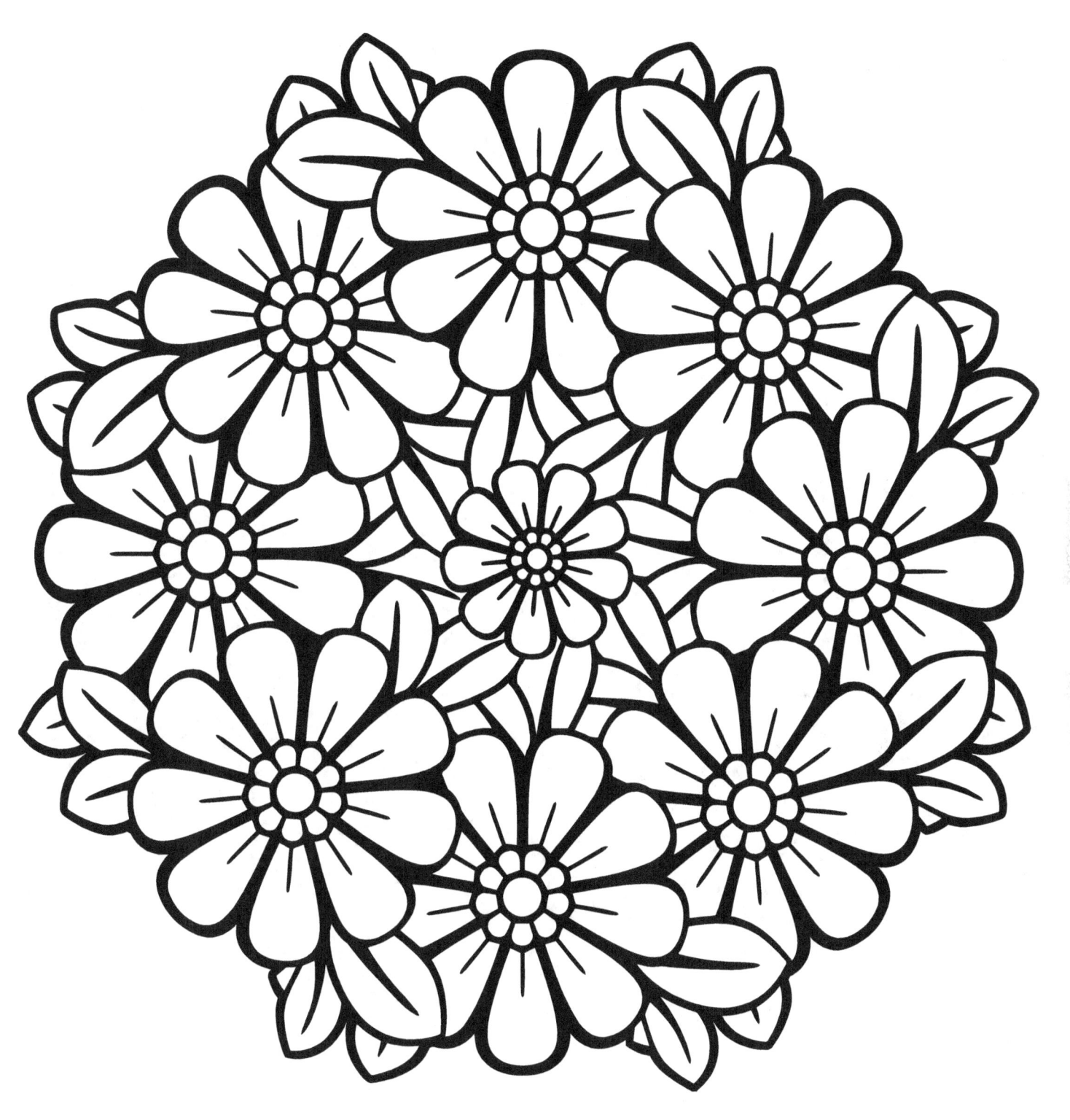

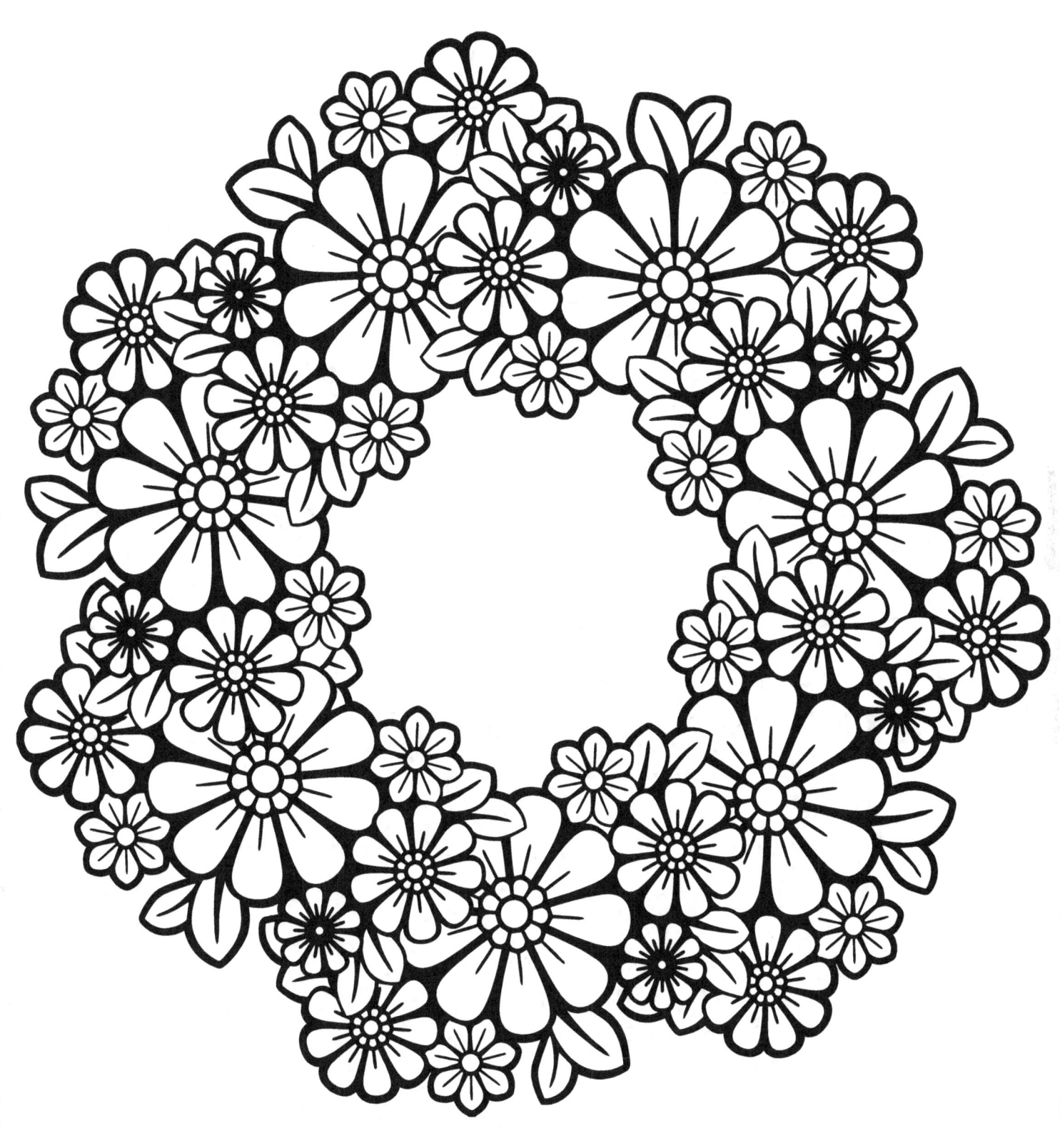

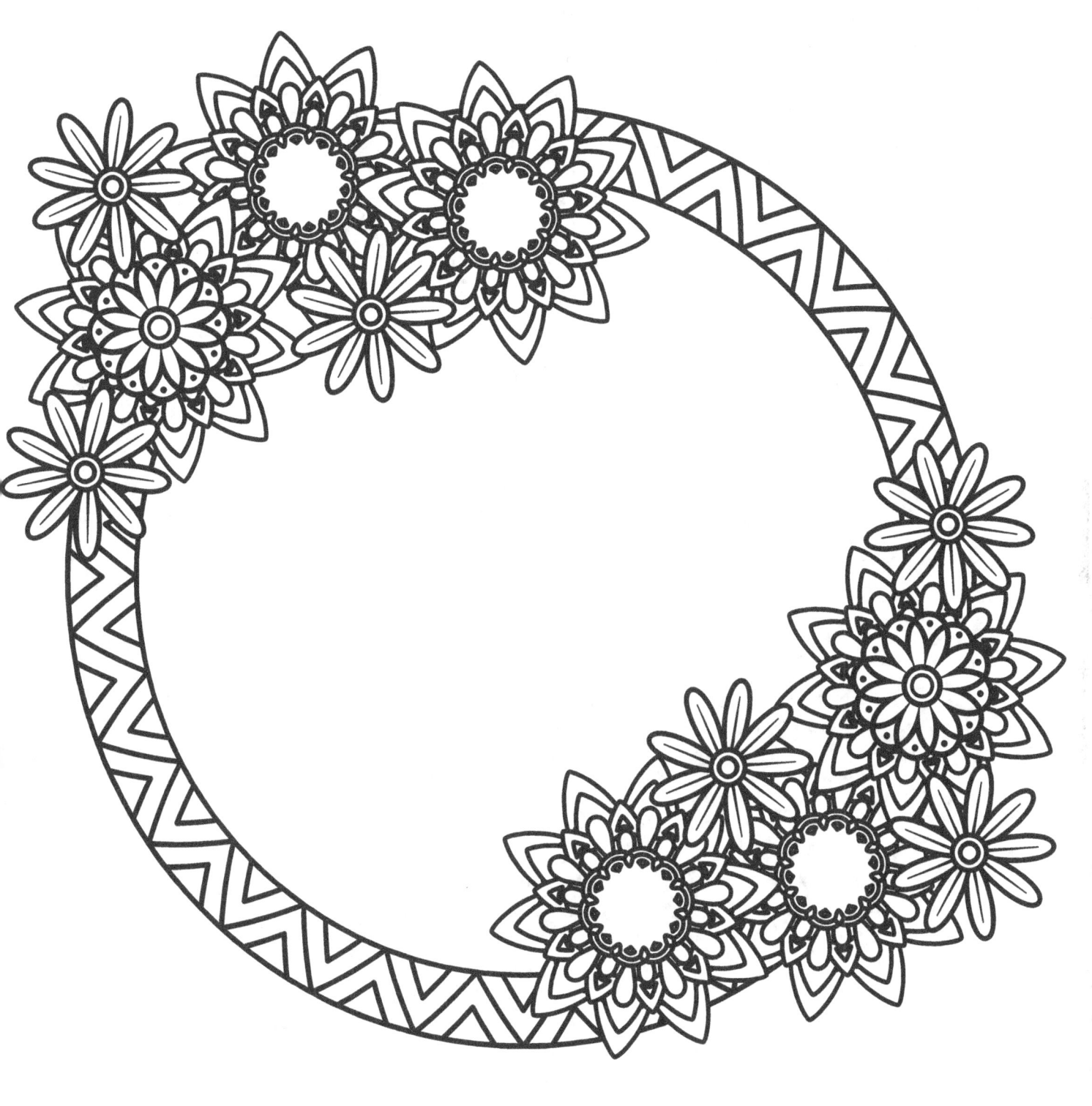

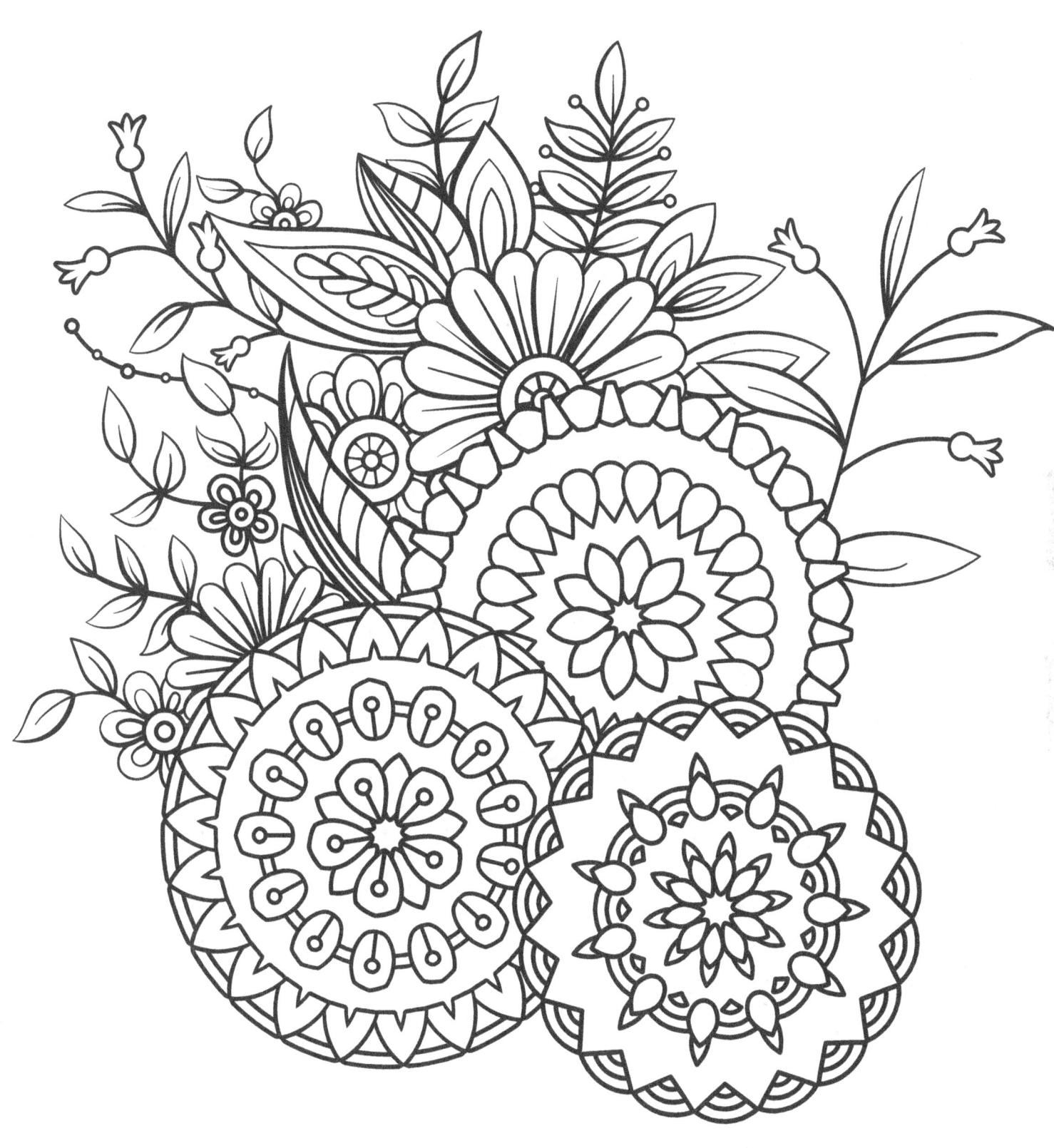

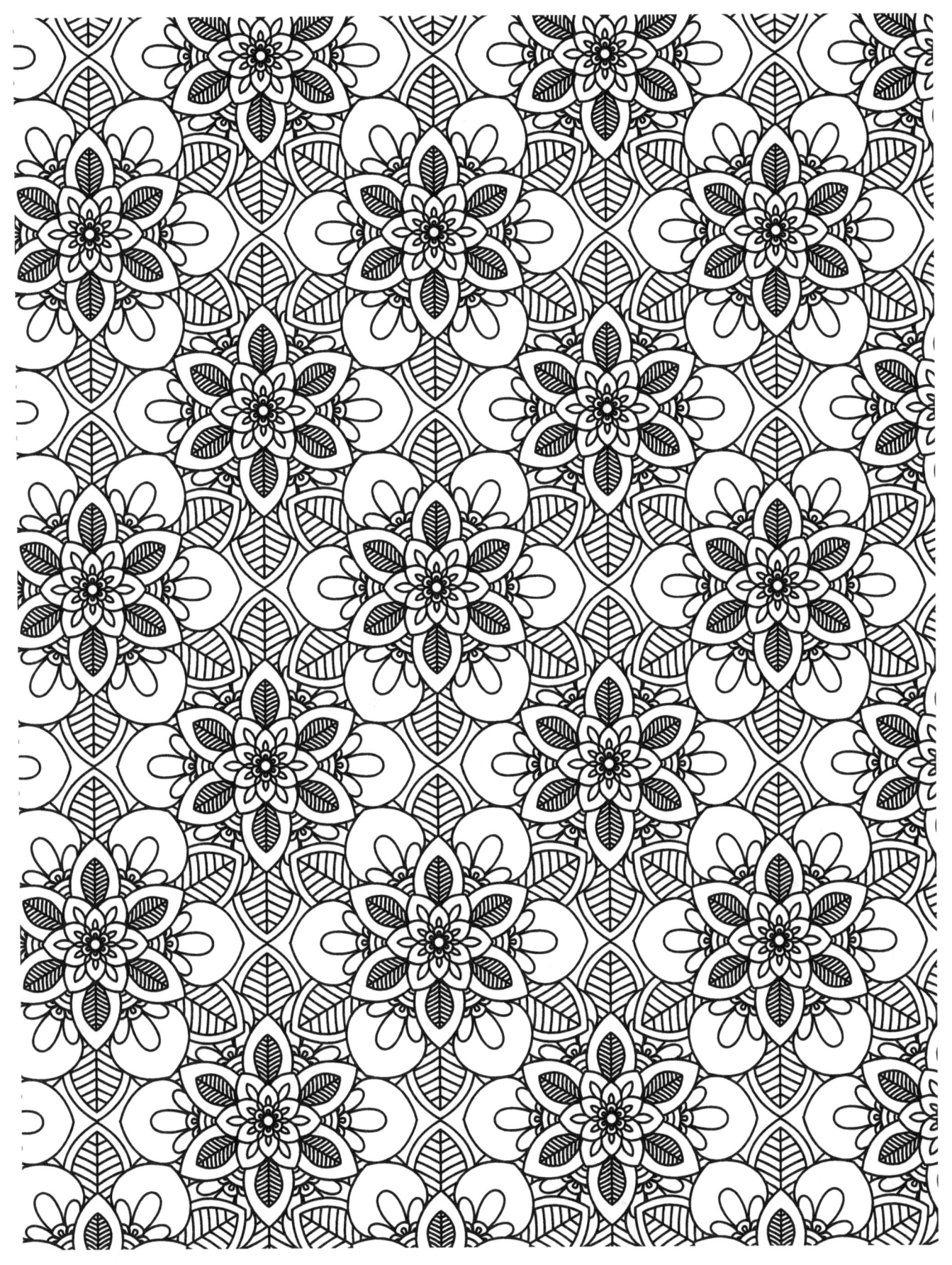

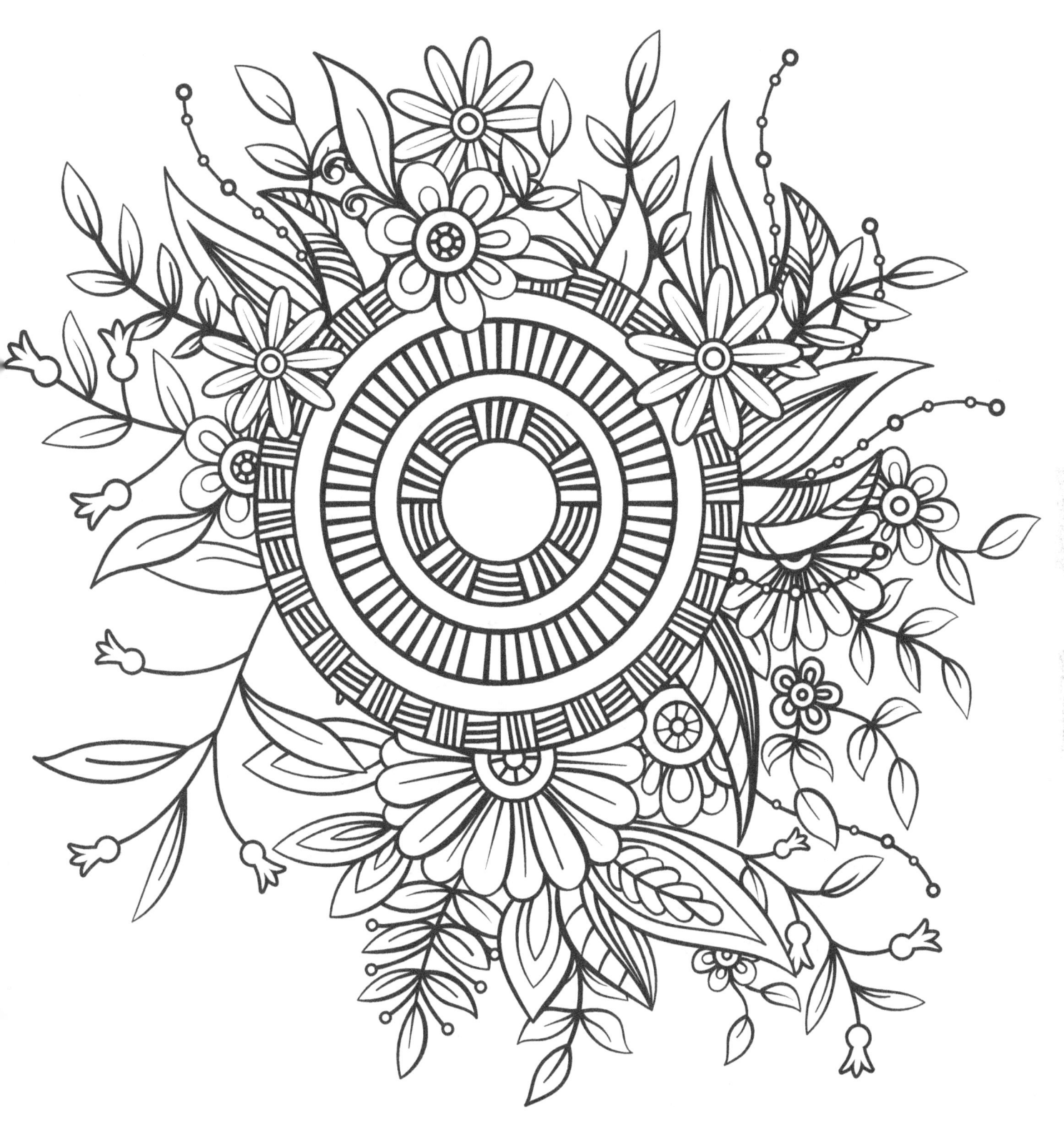

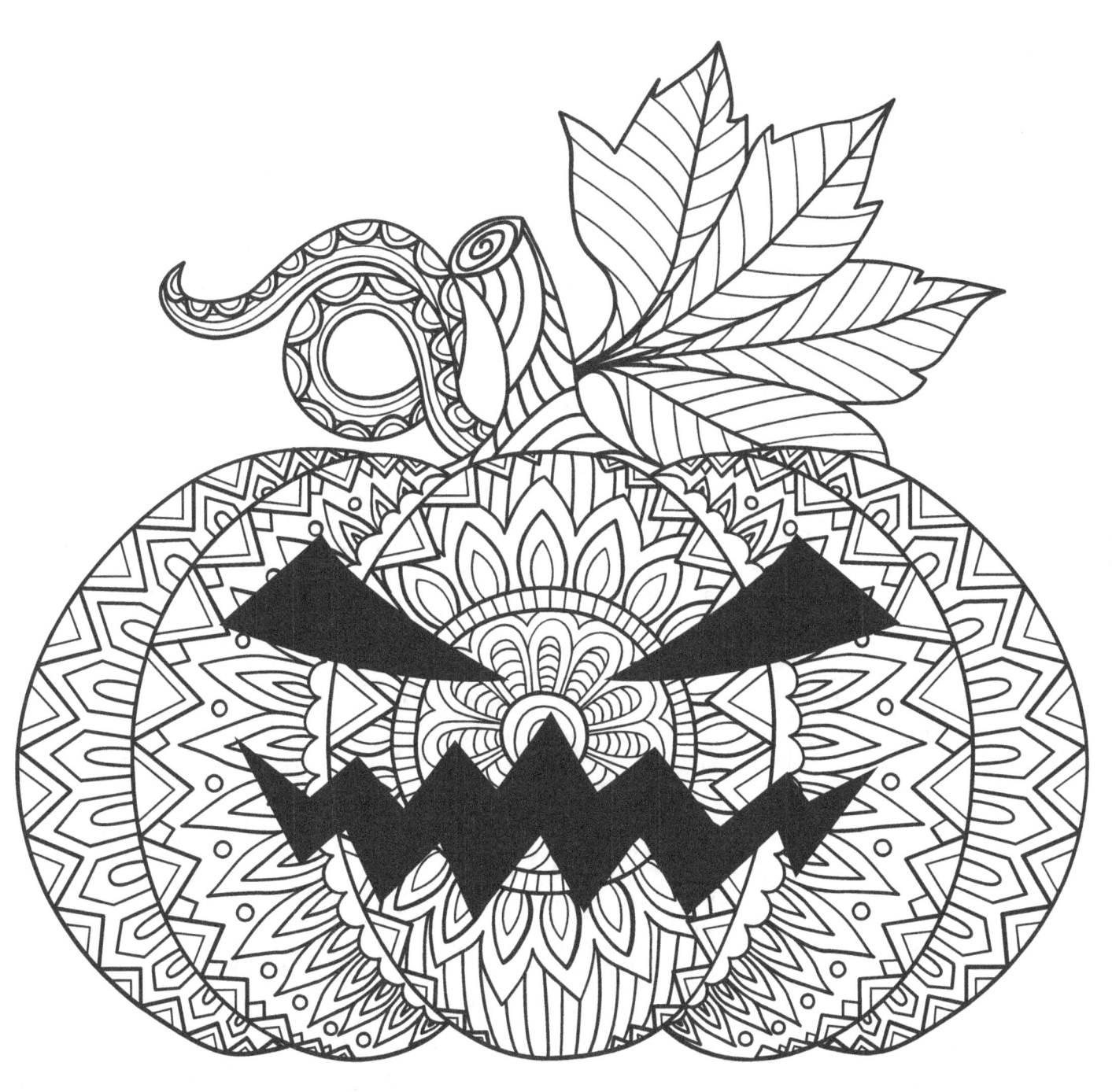

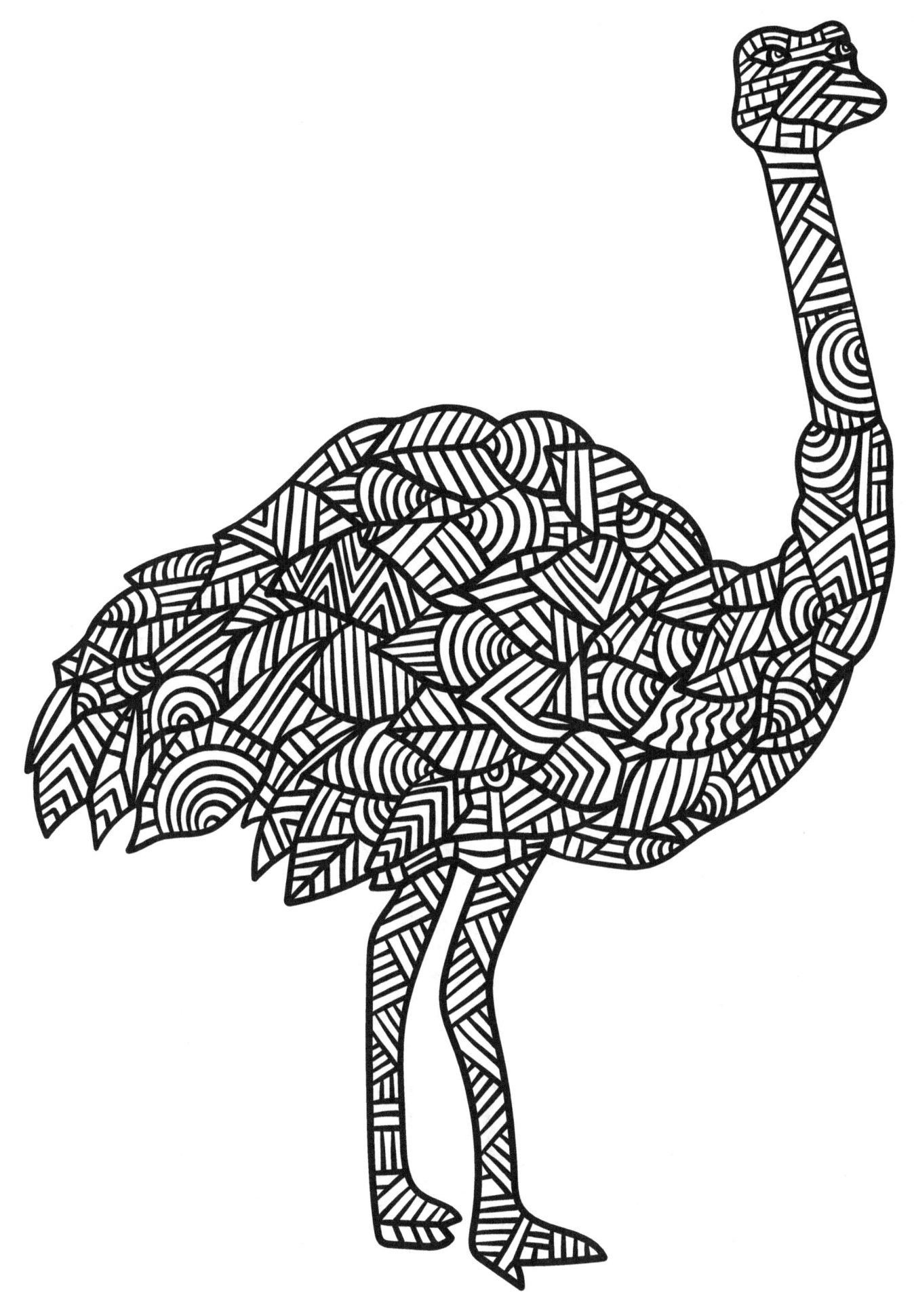

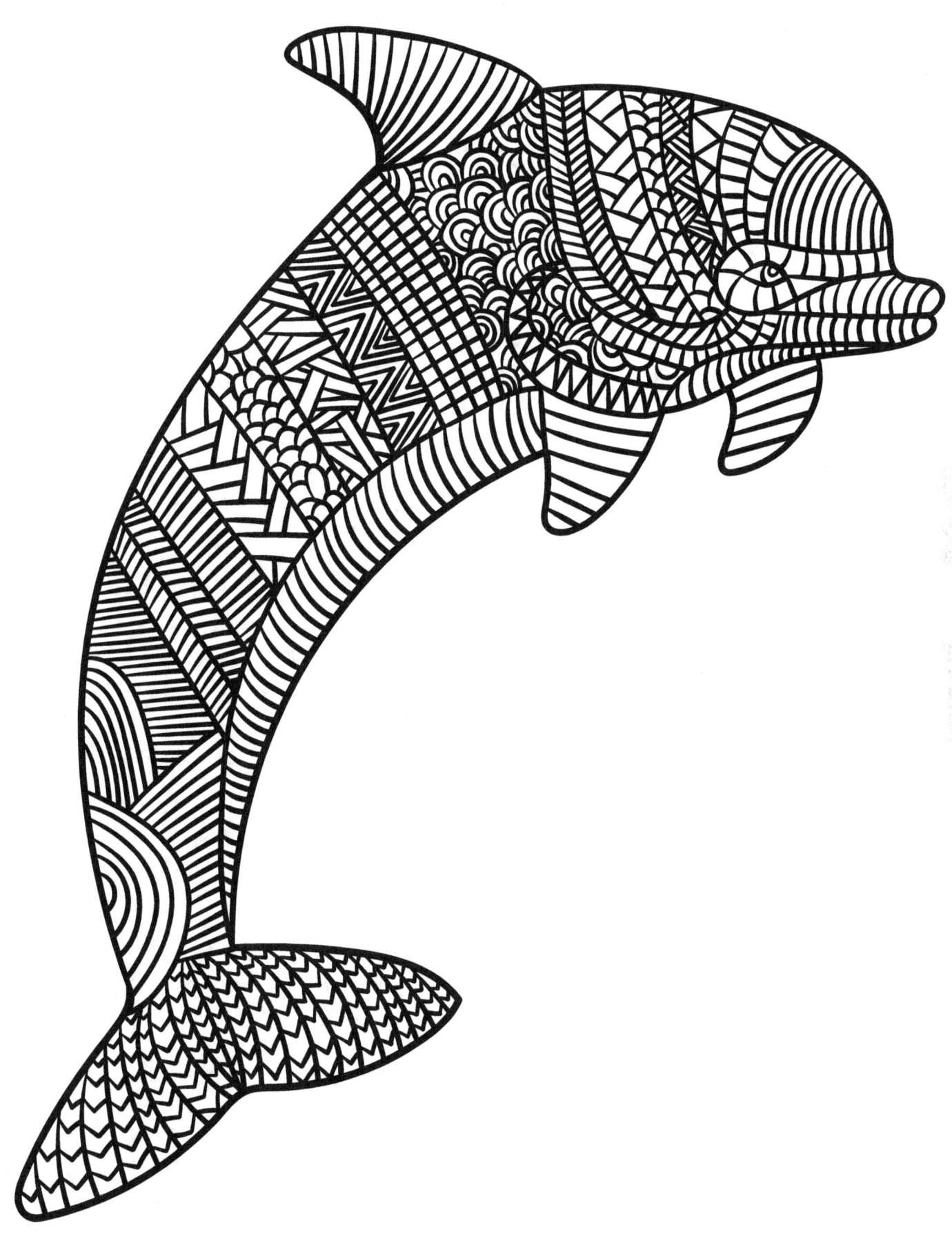

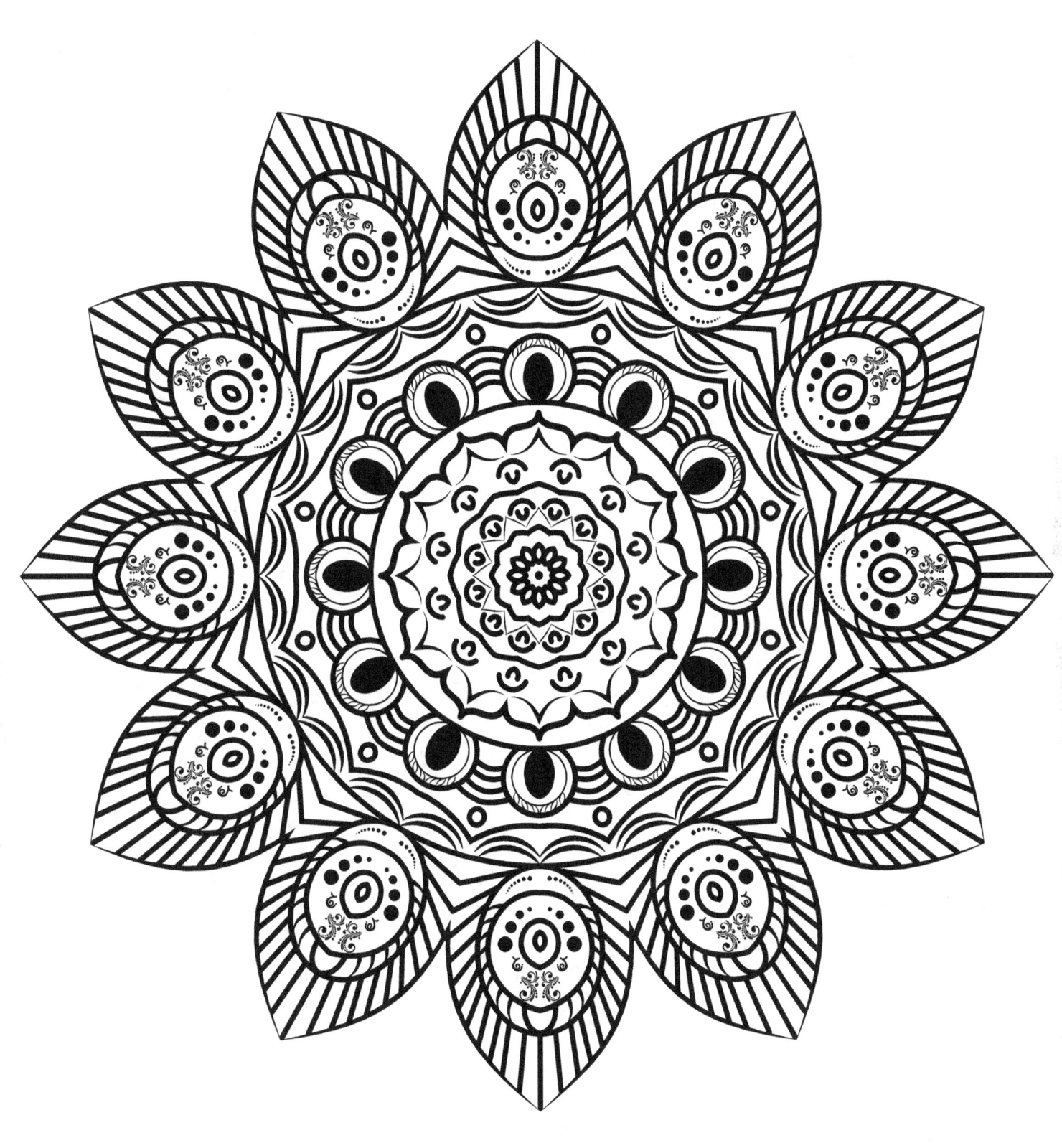